THE REAL READER'S QU

Slightly Foxed

'A Cheerful Revolutionary'

NO.51   AUTUMN 2016

Editors Gail Pirkis & Hazel Wood
Marketing and publicity Stephanie Allen & Jennie Paterson
Subscriptions Alarys Gibson, Anna Kirk, Olivia Wilson & Katy Thomas

Cover illustration: Olivia Lomenech Gill, 'Vasalisa's Garden', watercolour & gouache on board, 36cm x 30cm

Olivia is a professional artist. In recent years she has also worked on illustration after being commissioned to design and illustrate a book for Michael and Clare Morpurgo with Templar Publishing. This was shortlisted for the Kate Greenaway Medal in 2014 and nominated for the International Biennale of Illustration in Bratislava. Olivia lives and works in Northumberland, with her husband, a paper conservator, with whom she shares a dedicated print and conservation studio. For more information please visit: www.oliviagill.com or www.lomenechgill.com.

Design by Octavius Murray

Layout by Andrew Evans

Colophon and tailpiece by David Eccles

Published by Slightly Foxed Limited
53 Hoxton Square
London N1 6PB

tel 020 7033 0258
fax 0870 1991245
email all@foxedquarterly.com
www.foxedquarterly.com

Slightly Foxed is published quarterly in early March, June, September and December

Annual subscription rates
(4 issues plus digital access to all issues)
UK and Ireland £40; Overseas £48

Single copies of this issue can be bought for £11 (UK) or £13 (Overseas)

All back issues in printed form are also available: for details please ring 020 7033 0258
or visit our website www.foxedquarterly.com

ISBN 978-1-906562-89-2
ISSN 1742-5794

Printed and bound by Smith Settle, Yeadon, West Yorkshire

Contents

Contents

Ian Stephens, 'Tawny Owl',
wood engraving

From the Editors

After the events of the past few months, we must admit that, though extremely cheerful and optimistic, we're also feeling a bit ruminative here in the office. Somehow the timeless and civilizing things we hope *Slightly Foxed* stands for seem more important than ever at a moment of change like this. We hope, anyway, that with the arrival of this autumn issue you can relax, draw the curtains – actual or metaphorical – and, as one of our American readers recently described it, 'breathe a sigh of relief and slip into a world of thoughtfulness and good humor'.

Certainly there's nothing like reading about the past – perhaps especially the recent past – to give a steadying sense of perspective, and for this the latest of the Slightly Foxed Editions comes highly recommended. Anthony Rhodes's *Sword of Bone* (see p.14) is both an entertainment and an indictment of the waste and futility of war. Commissioned into the Royal Engineers on the eve of the Second World War, Rhodes found himself hanging about in France during the period of the Phoney War, requisitioning materials to extend the supposedly impregnable Maginot Line along the Belgian border as far as the coast. The situation had all the elements of a French farce, but when the Germans finally broke through and dive-bombed the retreating British Expeditionary Force on the beaches at Dunkirk, the laughter was over. It's a most unusual war book by an observant and cool-headed man who responded to even the most desperate situations with an ironic sense of humour.

For younger readers – and many nostalgic older ones too – Ronald Welch's Carey novels, the first twelve books in our Slightly Foxed

Cubs series, written between 1954 and 1972, take a long view of British history, following one family from the Crusades to the First World War and joining up the chronological dots in an extraordinarily lively way. Fast-paced and colourful, this is children's fiction of the best kind, rich in meticulously researched period detail and with real historical characters woven into the stories.

The final two books in the series are now available – *Ensign Carey*, which follows the fortunes of a hard-up Carey cousin from the gambling dens of mid-nineteenth-century London to the horrors of the Indian Mutiny, and *Tank Commander*, which takes the family story up to Britain's mobilization in the summer of 1914 and the eventual transformation of an apparently hopeless situation by the introduction of the tank. You'll find more details in the enclosed catalogue.

For any of you with gaps in the series, now is a good time to fill them while we still have stock – since these are limited editions we won't be reprinting. And looking ahead – as we know many of you do – the Carey series would make a very special present for a grandchild or godchild this Christmas. A reminder too that we now offer a special *SF* subscription rate of £28 to anyone under the age of 28, which comes with free digital access to all our past issues. It's a great way for young people to explore the world of books, for which there is no substitute, so do put the word out to anyone you think might be interested.

Last year we offered *Slightly Foxed* readers the opportunity to acquire a personalized yet affordable bookplate featuring a wood engraving by Howard Phipps. Those bookplates are still available but this year we are delighted to add four more designs by another of our favourite wood engravers, Sue Scullard. And finally, our new foxy Christmas card is now available, as is next year's *Slightly Foxed* calendar, featuring some of our favourite seasonal covers. Here's to some good things to write on it in 2017.

GAIL PIRKIS & HAZEL WOOD

A Cheerful Revolutionary

AMANDA THEUNISSEN

'Oh please, Nurse, tell me again how the French came to Moscow!' This was a constant petition of mine, as I stretched myself out in my crib . . .

'You were still with your foster mother; you were very small and weak then,' and I smiled with pride at the thought I had taken a part in the Great War.

Alexander Herzen was a nineteenth-century Russian political reformer and philosopher who wrote five volumes of what he described as 'memoirs in progress'. These are the opening lines of *Childhood, Youth and Exile* – the first two volumes of the sequence *My Past and Thoughts* – which covers his early years, 1812 to 1840. The other three volumes carry on from there and end around 1868.

The thread running through them is Herzen's turbulent, often tragic life and the terrible times – so far, so standard gloomily Russian – but they are unlike any other books of the era. Neither straightforward biography nor philosophical treatises, they're an entrancing mixture of personal recollections, political observations, social life in various countries, travel, economics, sharp comments on friends and enemies, and thoughts about Russia's past and future, all interspersed with extraordinary digressions and individual stories. Every now and

---

Alexander Herzen's five-volume memoir, translated as *My Past and Thoughts* (1861–7), is out of print, as is *Childhood, Youth and Exile* which was also published as a separate volume. However, the memoir is available in a print-on-demand format.

then Herzen breaks off the narrative to say 'In this context I must tell you what happened to . . .' and a story follows. It may be about the mad count who fed his guests on dog pie, or the vicious Governor of Siberia who, uniquely, was sacked for his brutality, or the honest doctor who let a thief go, or the disasters that befell his father's bailiff, or the Muslim Tartar who forcibly converted the pagan Finns to Russian Orthodoxy. Herzen describes nineteenth-century Russian life in a way no one else does, with a modern lightness of touch, acute observation, energy and wit I find irresistible.

Russian scholars know about Alexander Herzen but hardly anyone else seems to. He was a journalist who founded the first free Russian press in Europe and a prescient and influential political thinker, sometimes called the Father of Russian Socialism. For nearly thirty years he was a pivotal figure in Russian revolutionary politics, advocating emancipation of the serfs and an agrarian socialist society based on land reform. There were celebrations in Russia on the hundredth anniversary of his birth, when even the exiled Lenin gave him grudging endorsement while denouncing him as a petty-bourgeois socialist who didn't understand the reality of the class struggle. Tolstoy on the other hand said he'd never met anyone with 'so rare a combination of scintillating brilliance and depth'.

Herzen has two famous modern supporters – Isaiah Berlin, the Oxford philosopher, who wrote the illuminating introduction to my edition and saw Herzen as one of the great thinkers of history, and Tom Stoppard, whose trilogy *The Coast of Utopia* features Herzen and many of his revolutionary friends. It opened at the National Theatre in 2002 and on Broadway in 2007 but it's not one of Stoppard's best-known sets of plays and is hardly ever revived. Yet with two such eminent fans – and me – why is Herzen the forgotten revolutionary? It's time to rescue him from undeserved oblivion.

Alexander Ivanovitch Herzen was born in Moscow in 1812 and died in France in 1870. He was the illegitimate son of Ivan Yakovlev, a wealthy and well-connected Russian nobleman, and his German mistress. His father brought his mother to live in Moscow but never married her and, although Herzen inherited his fortune, he was never legitimized. He was, in short, a real Pierre Bezukhov. His childhood was difficult to say the least. His parents lived in separate parts of the same ghastly, lonely house. He was simultaneously ignored and mollycoddled – was 7 before he could go down the stairs unsupervised, at 15 wasn't allowed out alone, and until he was 21 had to be home by 10.30. He had no friends except the servants, and saw few people other than his parents and uncles.

His mother he hardly speaks of; his father might have been a model for Charles Ryder's father in *Brideshead Revisited* – clever, mean, selfish, disappointed and cold. He disapproved of all spontaneity or show of emotion, and could never understand why he had no friends. (His son grew up the opposite – impulsive, vivid and original, bursting with a humane joie de vivre.) His father never, says Herzen, ever did anything to oblige other people.

> His contempt for mankind was unconcealed without exceptions. Stinging mockery and cool contemptuous irony were the weapons he could wield with the skill of an artist but . . . who did he mean to impress by the performance? A woman whose will he had broken . . . a boy whom his own treatment drove from mere naughtiness to positive disobedience, and a score of footmen whom he did not reckon as human beings.

Russia in the nineteenth century was a terrible place – poor, undeveloped, brutal, venal and corrupt from top to bottom. There was no justice at any level. Nobles could buy their way out of trouble; the bribery continued on a descending scale until it reached the serfs, who were owned by their masters and had no rights. The Tsar, Nicholas I, had set up the Third Section, a prototype KGB, that sniffed out rebellion everywhere. Where they couldn't find it, they made it up, and the so-called courts meted out severe punishments. Once Herzen got to university (and even then he had to take a servant with him to lectures) he flourished – writing, drinking and dreaming of a new and better socialist Russia. And talking endlessly. Pavel Annenkov, a contemporary, wrote that he was almost overwhelmed by Herzen's 'extraordinary mind which darted from one topic to another with unbelievable swiftness, with inexhaustible wit and brilliance. He had the most astonishing capacity for instantaneous, unexpected juxtaposition of quite dissimilar things . . . You had to be prepared to respond instantly. All pretentiousness, all pedantic self-importance simply melted like wax before a fire.' Mind you, Annenkov added, 'I knew people, serious practical men, who could not bear Herzen's presence' – so maybe he makes for easier reading than listening.

As soon as he graduated in 1834 he was arrested by the Third Section, imprisoned, tried and sentenced to internal exile in Kirov. His crime – possibly singing anti-monarchist songs at a student party he could prove he had not attended. Russian justice in those days ran on sentence-first, verdict-afterwards lines. Many of his close friends suffered the same fate, and some did not survive. Herzen coolly writes that he preferred being in prison, where he could think in peace, to small-town Kirov, where he was surrounded by incompetents and dullards.

Childhood, Youth and Exile ends with his return to Moscow in 1840. Ahead lay even more turbulent years. Having inherited his father's fortune and married his cousin Natalie, in 1847 he left for France. Along went Natalie, three children, his mother, a tutor, a nanny and two servants. None of them ever set foot in Russia again. His closest friend, Nicholas Ogarev, and his wife (another Natalie who was also Herzen's mistress and bore him another three children) joined them.

In 1848 he experienced the heady excitement of that year's French revolution and its disappointing aftermath. Personal tragedy struck. He lost his wife, his mother and his son and in 1852, sad and disillusioned, he moved to England to lick his wounds. He didn't much care for London. He never learned to speak English properly (Jane Carlyle said his English was unintelligible), thought the women ugly and the men boring. However, he admired British institutions, particularly the legal system and the general tolerance of ideas.

In London he founded the Free Russian Press and published *Kolokol* (*The Bell*), probably the most effective crusading, muckraking newspaper ever. Written in Russian and aimed at everyone concerned with the future of the country, it uncovered and published stories of corruption, violence and injustice. It was astonishingly influential, read by everyone from, so people said, the Tsar downwards. Herzen's outlook was that of a modern campaigner. Publicity is the great weapon, he insisted – name and shame, and things will be done. In a prolix world he understood the value of the soundbite: 'Houses for free men cannot be built by specialists in prison architecture' hits the spot even now.

Basically Herzen was a socialist with a thick anarchic streak, a sceptical idealist. He passionately advocated an agrarian revolution and he campaigned for trial by jury and freedom of the press. Some part of all these reforms was granted by the new Tsar, Alexander II. Herzen was against nobles, rulers, politicians, judges, officials, police, most institutions and priests of all denominations, and in favour of people of goodwill, energy and honesty who want to change the world. But reform had to come from below, he insisted: the time had come to stop 'taking the people for clay and ourselves for sculptors'.

He wasn't a naïve dreamer; he understood the reality that revolutions consume themselves and he knew how easily men exchange one tyranny for another. Astonishingly prescient, while he feared the oppressors he feared the liberators just as much. As Isaiah Berlin says, 'He is terrified of them because for him they are the secular heirs of the religious bigots of the ages of faith; because anybody who has a cut and dried scheme, a straitjacket which he wishes to impose on humanity as the sole possible remedy for all human ills, is bound to create a situation intolerable for free human beings.'

Herzen met his fellow exile Marx in London. I thought they might have had convivial coffees together in Soho, discussing revolutionary theories, but in fact the air between them was thick with mutual dislike and distrust. Marx's grand theory that binds history, progress and the individual to some overarching abstraction was the antithesis of what Herzen believed. Another social reformer once said to him that man must always sacrifice himself to society.

'Why?' I asked.

'But surely the whole purpose and mission of man is the wellbeing of society?'

'But it will never be attained if everyone makes sacrifices and nobody enjoys himself!'

That's why, for me personally, Herzen is such an important figure. I was quite politically naïve when I first read him, sure the world was divided into Them and Us: the privileged and powerful on one side and Us on the other. I was bowled over by finding a serious writer who seemed to agree. He's an infinitely more sophisticated thinker than I could ever be but he laid the foundations of all my subsequent political beliefs then and I've never found reason to seriously doubt him. He supports the individual over the collective, the actual over the theoretical every time. What he really hated was the idea that some future blissful state justified present sacrifice and bloodshed; that people must endure terrible suffering now for some possible wondrous time ahead. Life was for living, he said, the present was what mattered, the future belonged to us, not we to it. He is the antidote to the gloomy Marx and the didactic Lenin. With courage and gaiety Herzen faced a world where, he said, nothing was certain, everything was possible and 'only art and the summer lightning of personal happiness' could be counted on.

When I took my copy off the shelf to write this piece, it fell apart. I have no idea where or when I acquired it – it's a paperback, printed in 1980, it cost £2.50 second- or third-hand, and to me it's a treasure. Herzen's wisdom, humanity and wit shine out from its battered pages. You only have to look at the world around us to see how right he was. And he straddles one of the most turbulent centuries in history. Napoleon had just entered Moscow when he was born in 1812. His father met the Emperor and got a free family pass out of the flames in exchange for taking a message to the Tsar. Aged 6, he debated loyalty and nationalism with an elderly French general who had been dining at Versailles in 1789 when Marie Antoinette raised her glass, toasting confusion to the French Revolution. His youngest daughter lived until 1920. From hoops, powdered hair and the guillotine to modern times in one giant stride. Add an unshakeable belief in individual freedom and human decency and the importance of having fun – how can such a man be forgotten?

AMANDA THEUNISSEN is a television producer who would like to be a serious political thinker but spends too much time trying to have fun.

Hanging Out on the Maginot Line

MICHAEL BARBER

In.1989 I was commissioned to write and present a programme about the Phoney War for BBC Radio 4. My research took me to the Imperial War Museum's sound archives and the testimony of a Dunkirk veteran called Anthony Rhodes, who was commissioned into the Royal Engineers shortly before Britain declared war on Nazi Germany in September 1939. At that stage I'd no idea Rhodes had written a book about his experiences, but what he had to say on tape was exemplary.

For instance, on arrival in France Rhodes and his comrades were shocked to discover that the impregnable Maginot Line did not extend along the Belgian frontier to the Channel. So if the Germans overran Belgium, as they had in 1914, there was nothing between them and the British Expeditionary Force (BEF), based near Lille, but a line of barbed wire. On the other hand Rhodes, like most Britons, was confident that the 'mighty' French Army, in alliance with the BEF, was more than a match for the Wehrmacht. Hitler had only been in power for six years. It took far longer than that to create a modern army from scratch. No wonder people said that the German tanks one saw in newsreels were made of cardboard!

Of course Rhodes was speaking retrospectively, but he didn't give the impression of being wise after the event. This was confirmed when I began to read his memoir *Sword of Bone*, the existence of which I learned about from a member of the museum's staff. It opens with a bombastic pep-talk by a general that does nothing to dispel what Rhodes calls his 'Passchendaele' notions of war. He had nightmares about trench warfare, 'the lowest and meanest form of life to which man has ever been ordered to sink'. But instead of wading through mud under shellfire he took part in that bizarre interlude known as the Phoney War, when it really was all quiet on the Western Front and Rhodes was mocked by a padre, of all people, for refusing a third cocktail before lunch in the front line. Then, in May 1940, not long after the Prime Minister Neville Chamberlain declared that Hitler had 'missed the bus', it became all too apparent that he hadn't. Within a few weeks Rhodes was literally burying his head in the sands of Dunkirk, a target for the Stukas and Messerschmitts overhead.

If Rhodes recoiled from the prospect of trench warfare this was not simply because it was so horrible. It was also because he and his contemporaries had been told that never again would the British Army be mired in such an aberrational conflict as the Great War, which ran contrary to military practice as the War Office understood it. 'Thank God that's over,' a British general is supposed to have said in 1919, 'now we can get down to some real soldiering again.' By 'real soldiering' he meant a small professional army engaged in regimental duties, recreations like polo and occasional skirmishes on the north-west frontier of India, a country to which the Army had an almost mystical attachment.

Real soldiering suited the Treasury, too. The cost of maintaining a huge army on the continent for four years had almost beggared Britain. It had no wish to repeat the experiment. But when, in March 1939, German troops entered Prague, the British government reluctantly concluded that Hitler could not be appeased. Conscription was reintroduced and it was obvious that sooner rather than later the Army would have to cross the Channel and once more 'do its bit'.

Born in 1916, Rhodes had spent his early years in India, where his father, a regular soldier, was on the Viceroy's staff. After Rugby School he entered the Royal Military Academy, Woolwich, where officer cadets destined for the Royal Artillery and the Royal Engineers were trained. He then read mechanical sciences at Trinity College,

Cambridge, graduating in 1939. Most young officers did not go to university then and by the time he graduated Rhodes's horizons were far broader than those of the average subaltern. He invokes Balzac, quotes Herrick and Goldsmith, and is even familiar with the concept of *feng shui* some forty years before it became a fad in the West.

Sword of Bone – the title is from Milton's *Samson Agonistes* – was first published in 1942, the same year that Richard Hillary's *The Last Enemy* appeared. Rhodes and Hillary, near contemporaries, had a lot in common. Both enjoyed experience for its own sake and were unimpressed by slogans and proprieties. For instance Rhodes is frank about the Army's use of brothels, something the brass hats tried to keep under wraps for fear of demoralizing wives and sweethearts at home, and he has an amusing anecdote about the confusion that arose from there being red lights over the doors of doctors' houses in north-east France. His tone of voice, like Hillary's, is tolerant, sceptical and ironic. Of a suave French liaison officer he writes: 'He had the air of having lived permanently at Prunier's, and of having drunk more cocktails than were good for him; all the signs, in fact, of a civilized man.' Another mark of a civilized man is his desire to live in peace. Even so, Rhodes did not expect to find, on a visit to the Maginot Line, that there existed an unofficial truce between its defenders and the Germans opposite.

Of course not everyone wanted to live and let live, a prime exception being Rhodes's divisional commander, a 'dynamic little man of obvious compressed energy' who was said, rather ominously, to be a glutton for punishment. Despite this, he was immensely popular not only with the troops but also with the Press. Although unidentified, this is clearly Montgomery. And since he was more than two years away from becoming a household name, it was percipient of Rhodes to single him out.

Conscious of how vulnerable they were to a German attack through Belgium, the British began to construct anti-tank ditches and pillboxes, the material for which it was Rhodes's job to purchase.

He was rarely in one place for long, which adds spice to his narrative. He thought Paris in the spring of 1940 had never been lovelier, his eye for a pretty girl, which more than one reviewer noted, given free rein. How appropriate, then, that he should learn that the war had begun in earnest from a young woman whose figure, her maid had assured him, was breathtaking:

> It must have been about six o'clock on the morning of May the 10th when my bedroom door was opened so violently that I woke; and my mind, still wandering in its own personal no man's land, had barely time to register the quick, fluttering movement of a form that passed the bed and alighted near the window. It was in this way that I was able to see Mlle Wecquier for myself. She was wearing a silk nightdress and, charmingly situated against the rays of the sun, her figure justified all that Marie had said of it . . . 'Lieutenant,' she said quite simply, 'we have been invaded.'

Alas for the Allies the Germans bypassed the Maginot Line and attacked through the supposedly impenetrable Ardennes forest, the defence of which had been just as neglected as the Belgian frontier. Within two weeks they had reached the English Channel, pulverizing the French with their blitzkrieg tactics and outflanking the BEF, who had no sooner dug in along the bank of the Belgian river Dyle than they were ordered to retire (the word 'retreat', as Rhodes reminds us, was never used in the British Army). So began 'a strategic withdrawal according to plan' that ended two weeks later at Dunkirk.

Rhodes and his unit were astonishingly lucky. Somehow they managed to evade the marauding columns of German tanks that caused such havoc, fortifying themselves en route to the coast with looted delicacies like foie gras washed down with champagne. His account of their progress is a bit like a Shakespearean battle: the fighting takes place offstage. At one point there's a surreal episode involving an arty brother officer of Rhodes's called Stimpson who insists on trying to replace the clarinet he's lost. 'He wants to pick one up *bon marché*,' Rhodes explains to a suspicious gendarme. For many of the civilians they met it was history repeating itself. The madame of a local brothel who'd always watered their drinks is philosophical. While admitting she would miss the Tommies, she consoles herself with the thought that if the last war is anything to go by, she will get even more custom from the Germans: 'They are certainly the most regular. You can rely on them.'

On the beaches at Dunkirk
© Imperial War Museum

You could also, as Rhodes soon discovered, rely on the Germans to bomb Dunkirk so regularly every half hour that you could almost tell the time by them. The docks were a prime target, making evacuation from there impossible, and Rhodes was told to take his men to the beach where thousands of troops had one eye on the sky for bombers and the other out to sea for ships. Although applauding heroism, Rhodes had no time for heroics: 'The officially advocated behaviour of standing up and firing a Bren gun at the aeroplane, even when it is on top of you, was put into practice by two of our men, who were promptly riddled with bullets.' What he doesn't say is that he himself was wounded in the back by a bomb splinter and temporarily lost his hearing.

Eventually, after queuing for hours in water up to their waists, he and what remained of his men were picked up by a rowing boat and transferred, via a trawler, to a destroyer, in which they crossed the Channel. On arriving home they were treated as heroes. But Rhodes knew he had taken part in a débâcle. His polished, wry and really rather subversive memoir belongs to what George Orwell called 'unofficial history' – the kind that is ignored in textbooks and lied about in the Press. At a time when we take spin for granted and free speech is under threat it certainly deserves a fresh airing.

Anthony Rhodes saw no more action after Dunkirk. He was involved in camouflage and coastal defence work and was then sent to lecture in Canada and the United States, where he married a niece of the composer Gustav Mahler. This was not a success, and following a nervous breakdown he was invalided out of the Army in 1945. Ten years later, after taking a degree in Romance Languages at Geneva University and teaching at Eton, he decided to write full-time. He wrote novels, biographies and travel books but is probably best known as the author of a three-volume history of the Vatican in the twentieth century. At his death in 2004 he was described in an obituary as a 'cosmopolitan and well-connected man of letters'.

MICHAEL BARBER has written and broadcast about books for more than forty years. The author of biographies of Anthony Powell, Evelyn Waugh and Simon Raven, he is a regular contributor to *Slightly Foxed* and *The Oldie*.

Anthony Rhodes's *Sword of Bone* (320pp) is now available from *Slightly Foxed* in a new limited and numbered cloth-bound pocket edition of 2,000 copies (subscriber price: UK & Eire £16, Overseas £18; non-subscriber price UK & Eire £17.50, Overseas £19.50). All prices include post and packing. Copies may be ordered by post (53 Hoxton Square, London N1 6PB), by phone (020 7033 0258) or via our website www.foxedquarterly.com.

Strindberg's Island

KARIN ALTENBERG

In my early twenties I became an avid sailor. Whenever life seemed too complex I would turn to the sea – to the curative simplicity of sailing. I loved to be in the grasp of the elements and was thrilled by the way a tug here or a pull there would miraculously bring everything into fragile balance.

One early autumn, when life wasn't going exactly to plan, I joined two friends sailing around the Stockholm archipelago, the 20,000 islands and skerries that protect the approach to the Swedish capital from the Baltic. As afternoon sank into evening we set course for the outer islands and Kymmendö, the setting of August Strindberg's novel *The People of Hemsö (Hemsöborna)*.

Here and there they slipped past a broom beacon, sometimes a ghostly white sailing-mark, in some places late snowdrifts shone like linen on a bleaching green, in others net floats rose to the surface of the black water and scraped against the keel as the boat passed over them.

This is the passage that I remember best from my first reading of the novel: the approach to Hemsö. I must have read it when I was still at school, but the image of this peaceful night sail, where things seem to come alive in the dark, had settled in the shallows of my mind.

It was also an image that had stayed in Strindberg's imagination for many years. He wrote the novel in exile, during one of the darkest

August Strindberg, *The People of Hemsö* (1887)
Norvik Press · Pb · 164pp · £11.95 · ISBN 9781870041959

periods of his life. In 1884, in a letter to his publisher, he said: 'I need to go away to purge Sweden and Swedish stupidity from my system.' He spent the next three years travelling around Europe with his family. On reaching Lindau, on the shores of Lake Constance in Bavaria in 1887, misery finally caught up with him; his recent writings on Swedish life and society had made him unpopular – even hated – by conservatives and feminists alike. His publisher was getting increasingly nervous about his work, and his marriage to Siri von Essen had turned sour. Obsessed with the idea that his wife was unfaithful, he also worried that his penis might be too small. This was not a new anxiety for Strindberg but on this occasion he was 'irritated to the roots of my testicles' and resolved to get an expert opinion. In a letter that year he wrote cheerfully after a doctor's examination (in a brothel): 'I had my semen investigated which proved fertile, and was measured at full cock (16 x 4 centimetres).'

Far away, angry, paranoid and pursued, Strindberg was homesick. That autumn in Lindau, his manhood freshly measured, his mind turned to the island of Kymmendö, where he had spent so many happy summers, and he sat down to write a novel about life in the Swedish countryside and skerries, 'the first genuine novel I have written'. Remarkably *The People of Hemsö* shows no sign of a tortured mind. On the contrary, this is a novel full of life, humour and compassion, capturing the light and colour of the summer skerries. After the darkness of a long winter, summer illuminates the islands in full Technicolor. For the briefest of times the greenery seems greener and the sea and sky bluer than anywhere else in the world. Newly reborn, nature is so freshly minted it makes you feel almost unclean.

Strindberg, better known for his plays, wrote most lyrically about the islands in his poetry, but most successfully in *The People of Hemsö*. The plot is simple enough: Carlsson arrives on the island from the forests of the north to become factor at the farm of the widow Flod. Madame Flod's adolescent son, Gusten, is more interested in sailing around the skerries and shooting seabirds than managing the farm, and Carlsson soon sees an opportunity for advancement. Before long, Gusten is outmanoeuvred as Carlsson marries Madame Flod 'for the gold'. The wedding itself is a shambles, conducted by a drunken minister. The story is generally described as a naturalistic tragi-comedy or a burlesque, but Strindberg himself called it 'rustic realism' and wavered between thinking it a masterpiece and a farrago of caricatures.

The novel may be all of these things, but it is completely charming and quite unlike anything else he wrote. The exiled writer's love of 'home' is so present you begin to think it may be *your* home. More characteristically, perhaps, it is also a story of lust and power. As an outsider, Carlsson eventually finds that he cannot master his new environment. He is alone, and as a farmer from the north he remains a stranger in the seascape of the archipelago, whereas Gusten, the hunter and the son of the sea, rises to the task and triumphs.

The novel is also full of passages of breathtaking beauty, and its detailed descriptions document a traditional way of life in the skerries that would soon disappear with the introduction of tourism.

Conscious that his marriage was collapsing, the tormented Strindberg wrote of the bright joys of love on the summer island of Kymmendö, where he first brought his wife shortly after they were married, and where their first child, Greta, was christened. Ironically he was never to return. He had written his first play, *Master Olof*, there, having rented rooms from a former farmhand who had married the widowed mistress of the farm. When *The People of Hemsö* was published in 1887 his former hosts forbade him from ever setting foot on Kymmendö again.

The novel's first sentence is widely considered one of the most famous openings in Swedish literature. Only sixteen words long, it uses all nine vowels in the Swedish language, and most of the consonants, and a sea-breeze blows through the sentence and brings us straight into its seascape. (Strindberg excelled at jumping straight to the core in his opening sentences: 'Miss Julie's gone mad again tonight. Completely mad!') Unfortunately, it is almost impossible to catch that breeze in translation, though I shall try:

Han kom som ett yrväder en aprilafton och hade ett höganäskrus i en svångrem om halsen.
He came like a whirlwind on an April evening with a jug on a strap round his neck.

Four wonderful nouns set the sentence in motion – *yrväder* (whirlwind), *aprilafton* (April evening), *höganäskrus* (earthenware jug from Höganäs) and *svångrem* (strap). There is flurry and movement in Strindberg's writing and you sense both the threat of disorder and the energy of action – and the jug full of schnapps swinging from Carlsson's neck may also be an indication of things to come. The ever-present wind defines the seascape and blows life – and peril – into those who pass through it.

That autumn when I sailed to Kymmendö we berthed in darkness. The next morning I walked across the island to the north-east side and my place of pilgrimage: Strindberg's writing-hut. He built this tiny shack of unpainted pine planks with the aid of local farmhands in 1872. Weathered by wind and sun, it is empty now, but it has been lovingly preserved by the Strindberg Society. Inside, the pine-planks shivered, and through the single window facing the sea the sun was just shaking itself free of the horizon. At that moment the mirrored surface rippled in a sigh of morning breeze and the light exploded, shooting diamonds through the glass. Dazzled, I sat for a while on the rocks outside the hut and smelt the pine resin heating up in the woods behind me. Then I took off my clothes and went for one of the most perfect swims of my life.

KARIN ALTENBERG once sailed to St Kilda and survived. For this reason, perhaps, her latest novel, *Breaking Light*, is mainly landlocked. Recently she paddled up the Missouri River in search of a new story. Like Strindberg she is Swedish, but the comparison ends there.

The Rummidge Chronicles

HENRY JEFFREYS

The philosopher Roger Scruton refers to modern academia as the 'nonsense factory'. In a recent interview he bemoaned students 'clogging their minds with nonsense from Deleuze and Foucault when they could be reading Shakespeare'. This was very much my experience studying English literature at university in the 1990s. The lecturers, rather than imparting a great love of the classics, spouted half-digested bits of literary theory at us. I still shudder when I recall the tortured theorizing of writers such as Judith Butler (who won the *Philosophy and Literature* Bad Writing Contest in 1998 for a particularly incomprehensible sentence). Tutorials would consist of discussions of our lecturers' theories about theory. It was maddening.

Some fellow English literature students took refuge in drink, drugs or promiscuity. My escape was the novels of David Lodge. Between 1975 and 1988 he wrote *Changing Places*, *Small World* and *Nice Work*, which form a loose trilogy set mainly at Rummidge University, a very lightly fictionalized version of Birmingham where Lodge taught. The first novel, *Changing Places*, concerns an exchange programme where the stolid and unambitious Philip Swallow from Rummidge swaps with the dynamic, cynical Morris Zapp from Esseph University in the State of Euphoria (Lodge spent six months teaching at UC, Berkeley in the late '60s).

It is, I suppose, an experimental novel; parts are written in the form of letters, film scripts, flashbacks or newspaper clippings. Don't

David Lodge's *Changing Places* (1975), *Small World* (1984) and *Nice Work* (1988) are all available as Vintage paperbacks, each priced at £8.99.

let that put you off, though. It's really a classic fish-out-of-water tale, with the thrusting American baffled by backward Birmingham, and Philip embracing the freedom offered to him by America. Zapp is appalled by cold, pre-central heating England as well as the chilly reception in the English department: nobody talks to him for the first week. Swallow, in contrast, proves an immediate hit in America when he introduces the game 'Humiliation' at a faculty party. In it the participant has to name a literary work he hasn't read, and he gets a point for everyone else who has read it. The way to win the game is to show your ignorance in front of your peers, hence the title.

The sequel, *Small World*, takes the jet-setting of its predecessor to absurd lengths. There's a vast cast of characters and, instead of two campuses, it's set at conferences all over the world: in fact much of the action takes place in aeroplanes and airports. The subtitle 'An Academic Romance' gives a clue to the structure. A character defines romance as 'a pre-novelistic kind of narrative. It's full of adventure and coincidence and surprises and marvels', which is an apt summing up of the novel. It consists of a series of quests: the main hero Persse McGarrigle from Limerick pursues his love, Angelica Pabst, around the world while academics compete for that Holy Grail, the UNESCO Chair of Literature, which equals money, status and, best of all, no teaching.

Swallow and Zapp feature, of course, but what ties all the strands together is the Heath Robinsonesque plot where seemingly uncon-nected events – a publisher having an affair with his secretary, for example – have distant repercussions and Swallow becomes front-runner for the ultimate prize. It truly is a small world.

While reading *Small World* I thought to myself, who pays for all the jet-setting? The answer, at least in Britain, is the taxpayer, and the final part of the trilogy, *Nice Work*, looks at what happens when an academic goes out into the world of work. Dr Robyn Penrose is sent to shadow Vic Wilcox, manager of a Rummidge engineering firm. Swallow and Zapp have only minor roles this time, for in contrast to its predecessors, *Nice Work* is set in the more realistic world of 1980s Britain, where 'receiverships and closures have ravaged the area in recent years, giving a desolate look to the streets'. Of course Lodge still manages to have lots of fun by making Penrose an expert on Victorian literature and having her journey echo novels such as Elizabeth Gaskell's *North and South* while all the time she denies that literature can ever truly be 'realist'.

Indeed, one of the pleasures of these novels lies in spotting the literary references. Some are obvious, others less so. At one point in *Small World* McGarrigle stumbles into a street theatre version of *The Waste Land*, and his acquisition of his lectureship in a case of mistaken identity echoes Evelyn Waugh's *Scoop*. Lodge's warring academics and students are all steeped in literature. Swallow's game, 'Humiliation', only works because the protagonists are so well read. An elderly academic, Miss Maiden, says at one point: 'I respect a man who can recognize a quotation. It's a dying art.' One cannot imagine playing this now because people no longer have the same frame of references. (A friend of mine teaches a creative writing course and the only novel everyone on the course has read is *Fight Club* by Chuck Palahniuk.)

As well as being an escape, these novels echoed my own struggles with literary theory. Robyn Penrose forces her mind through 'the labyrinthine sentences of Jacques Lacan and Jacques Derrida until her eyes are bloodshot and her head aches'. I know that feeling. Robyn represents the new wave, the kind of lecturers who taught me at university, whereas Swallow is the old guard, concerned with the primacy of the author's voice and even believing in the moral power of literature. The trilogy charts the change in English literature from a study of great writers to a study of writers through the prism of theory or indeed just pure theory. Swallow says in *Small World*: 'There was a time when reading was a comparatively simple matter . . . Now it seems to be some kind of arcane mystery, into which only a small élite have been initiated.'

The few novelists who appear, such as Ronald Frobisher, a former Angry Young Man, and Zapp's estranged wife Désirée, are baffled and isolated by all the theorizing. 'They both feel intimidated by the literary jargon of their hosts which they both think is probably nonsense but cannot be quite sure.' Which is just how I felt.

Zapp, though of Swallow's generation, is happy to ride cynically on the back of whatever theory happens to be fashionable at the time: 'His style of teaching was designed to shock conventionally educated students out of a sloppy reverent attitude to literature and into an ice-cool, intellectually rigorous one.' This is almost exactly what we were told on day one of our English literature degree. The problem with this style of teaching is that it's only applicable to students with a good sound knowledge of literature. This didn't apply to most of my contemporaries; they hoped to be taught literature and instead they were taught irreverence for something they had never been reverent about. As a character in *Nice Work* puts it:

> The irony of teaching it [theory] to young people who have read almost nothing except a GCE set text and Adrian Mole, who know almost nothing about the Bible or classical mythology . . . the irony of teaching them about the arbitrariness of the signifier in week three of their first year becomes in the end too painful to bear.

These are not just novels of ideas, however. Lodge has a gift for characterization which is particularly apparent in *Small World*. Well-placed minor characters have strategically important roles and even the most minor characters are portrayed with warmth and flair. There's Fulvia Morgana, an Italian Marxist, who drives a gold Maserati and holds forth about 'the necessity of Revolution with her

Anna Trench

mouth full of sacher torte'. My particular favourites are the Turkish academics Akbil and Oya Borak, who studied in Hull. A lesser writer would use them as an excuse for some jokes at the expense of this much-maligned town. Instead, back in Turkey now, they miss their old life and on cold winter nights warm themselves with shared memories of Hull, 'murmuring the enchanted names of streets and shops, "George Street", "Hedon Road", "Marks and Spencer's"'.

Above all these are very funny novels. Much of the comedy comes from their self-awareness but you don't need to be an English litera-ture student to get all the jokes. When Morris Zapp is kidnapped by communists in *Small World* his wife Désirée tries to haggle with them over the ransom money. One of the concluding chapters of *Changing Places* contains a scene that's pure slapstick: Morris Zapp being chased around a paternoster lift by the increasingly unhinged head of English at Rummidge, Gordon Masters.

The first two novels also seem alarmingly prescient. There's a char-acter in *Changing Places*, Wily Smith, who pretends to be black and is writing a novel about the black experience. Esseph University is desperate to employ more black or Native American lecturers so that they don't seem racist. *Small World* presents a world transformed by technology: jet travel, direct-dial telephones and Xerox machines, the Internet of the 1970s. Only *Nice Work*, the most modern of the three, seems dated because it's so firmly rooted in Thatcher's Britain. It's also the only novel where you feel Lodge's own politics coming to the fore.

Nobody writes novels like these any more. The nearest thing in recent years was Zadie Smith's *On Beauty*. Which is a shame – just think how much fun one could have these days with 'no platforming' and 'safe spaces' at modern universities. Though perhaps student pol-itics nowadays are beyond parody; and of course the madness of academic theory has percolated into everyday life – Facebook has twenty-one terms to define your gender.

Though Lodge satirizes academia, he also loves it. It's his world, and theory is a game he knows how to play. *Small World* ends at the MFA, the daddy of all conferences, where a character says that what 'matters in the field of critical practice is not truth but difference. If everybody were convinced by your arguments, they would have to do the same as you and then there would be no satisfaction in doing it. To win is to lose the game.' Me, I managed to play well enough to get a decent degree. Still, in retrospect, I do wish I'd taken a principled stand against 'the nonsense factory'. It might have livened up those deadly tutorials.

After stints in the wine trade and publishing, HENRY JEFFREYS is now a writer specializing in drinks. He contributed to *The Breakfast Bible*, and his history of Britain told through drink, *Empire of Booze*, will be published in November.

Ian Stephens, 'Great Spotted Woodpecker',
wood engraving

WOOD ENGRAVERS III

For the third in our occasional series featuring the work of some of our favourite wood engravers we've chosen Ian Stephens. Ian was born in North Buckinghamshire in 1940. He studied illustration at Northampton School of Art and started engraving immediately on leaving. He has been an art teacher and, subsequently, a graphic designer and illustrator. He is now semi-retired but produces drawings for *The Jackdaw* and is still engraving. He can be contacted at 46 Yardley Drive, Northampton NN2 8PE or on 01604 460457. Sadly he is an e.dunce. Other examples of his work can be seen on pp. 4, 40, 57 and 74.

A Battersea Childhood

JEREMY LEWIS

Richard Church is remembered, if at all, as a late-flowering Georgian poet and a busy man of letters who contributed reviews to such long-forgotten periodicals as *John O'London's Weekly*, and who in due course became Dylan Thomas's baffled and increasingly embattled editor at J. M. Dent. But he deserves to be better known, if only for one book. Published by Heinemann in 1955, *Over the Bridge* is the first volume in an autobiographical trilogy (the other volumes of which were *The Golden Sovereign* and *The Voyage Home*); it takes him up to the age of 16, when he abandoned dreams of art school in favour of a career in the Civil Service, and it's a small masterpiece of autobiography.

Church grew up in the old town of Battersea, between Battersea Bridge and the eighteenth-century church on the river: it lay 'over the bridge' from fashionable Chelsea, and the book opens on New Year's Day 1900 with the 7-year-old Richard Church and his older brother gingerly carrying a fish-tank from an awe-inspiring artist's house in Tite Street to their house on the other side of the river, dodging a gang of urchins on the way. A low-lying area of mudflats and damp and sulphurous fogs, Battersea was 'a slumbrous suburb, largely peopled with artisan folk, clerks and minor Civil Servants such as my father' and an itinerant cast of muffin-men, lamp-lighters and pigeon-fanciers. It was a Wellsian, lower middle-class world, yet many of its inhabitants had surprisingly grand or distinguished

Richard Church, *Over the Bridge: An Essay in Autobiography* (1955), is out of print.

relations: Church's mother, a Midlands girl, was related to George Eliot; an elderly glazier turned out to be the brother of J. A. Froude, the eminent Victorian historian, while a military-looking commissionaire was the brother of General Hector Macdonald, a hero of the Boer War.

Unencumbered by important connections, Church's father occupied a humble position in the Post Office. Years before, boldly venturing over the river to Chelsea, he and a gang of boys couldn't resist pelting an irascible-looking Thomas Carlyle with pickled eggs in Cheyne Row – this was, Church observed, 'my father's only contact with the world of letters during his formative years' – and despite his bristling black moustache he remained a perpetual boy: his son remembered him as 'a creature released, like a colt from a stable', who 'galloped about the paddock of life with a thunder of hoofs and a flashing of nostrils'. Like many late Victorians and Edwardians, he was a passionate bicyclist, a 'knight of the wheel' who took to the open road at the slightest provocation, his lower half clad in spats and knickerbockers, and in due course he bought a couple of tandems so that his wife and two sons could join him in tours of the Home Counties. He also played the violin and the flute, specializing in homely and frequently repeated melodies, while his wife accompanied him on an elderly upright piano.

But for all Mr Church's energy and enthusiasm, his wife was – for their younger son at least – the epicentre of the family. An elementary schoolteacher by profession, she was passionate about her husband and her sons but suffered from ill-health and melancholia: Church, who was devoted to her, recalls her 'rich personality, her fearless ambitions, and her quick, intuitive intelligence', and 'the warm brown of her hair and eyes, the firm mouth, the blood-mantled cheeks, and the undecided conflict between joy and melancholy that affected every movement of her over-expressive features'. But the most forceful member of the family was Richard's older brother, Jack. An austere, domineering, rather monk-like figure, with a great beak of a nose and eyes that 'smouldered back in their caverns like panthers at bay', Jack seemed far cleverer and more talented than his nervous and late-developing younger brother: he was a brilliant pianist, scorning his father's middlebrow melodies in favour of Beethoven sonatas and insisting that the family piano be replaced with something more suited to his gifts, and a competent artist.

Poor Richard was, by contrast, an unimpressive specimen. Supersensitive and, one suspects, highly neurotic, he suffered from stomach cramps and was more allergic than most to noise. 'I was an apprehensive boy, groping my way through the world as a snail does, by the aid of instinctive horns that retracted with lightning speed before the least opposition,' he tells us, and 'what I lacked in intellectual fibre I made up in nervous sensibility. I thought through my skin, as a cat does.' Like many children, he believed he could fly if he really bent his mind to it, and he retained his faith longer than most. He was also extremely short-sighted – so much so that he enjoyed an almost mystical moment of revelation when an optician in Clapham fitted him out with a pair of specs. He immediately taught himself to tell the time, and before long he had learned to read.

The Churches were not a bookish family, but Richard was a natural bookworm. He worked his way through *Masterman Ready* at the age of 7, before moving on to the Book of Job. 'Only in reading did I find serenity and self-confidence,' he writes. 'As soon as I put my book down and took off the armour of words, I felt the winds of life blow cold upon my nakedness and I shivered with apprehension.' But reading could prove a fraught affair: he read *Villette* 'with an intensity of emotion that made the sweat stand in beads on my forehead and run down over my spectacles, so that I had to take them off and wipe them, while dipping my head closer into the book to continue reading with the naked eye'. Finding his way into print for the first time with a short story in the school magazine – 'Fine, my son. Stick to it!' his father told him, before pedalling off into the distance – made him 'vain and self-conscious (a weakness that I was later to find to be an occupational disease in the literary profession)'.

Richard was 11 when it was decided that his mother's health could stand the damp of Battersea no longer, and the family moved east to Herne Hill. Richard still 'hovered over life with as much certainty as a dragonfly over a brook on a hot day', but he was sent to a school in Dulwich where the headmaster recognized and encouraged his artistic gifts. A precocious reader, he immersed himself in Ruskin and worked his way through George Eliot's *Romola*; but above all he wanted to be a painter. He was offered a place at Camberwell Art School, but his father insisted that he should instead study for the Civil Service exams. He went to work in the Land Registry offices in Lincoln's Inn. Brother Jack became a schoolmaster, and *Over the Bridge* ends with young Richard keeping himself awake at night to read the books he might have read had he gone on to art school or university.

He was also writing poems, some of which found their way into print. In 1933 he abandoned the Civil Service for the literary life, and joined J. M. Dent as their poetry editor. Two years later, the young Dylan Thomas submitted a collection of poems to the firm. Church had no time for the work of T. S. Eliot or Gerard Manley Hopkins, and he regarded surrealism in poetry with abhorrence, telling Thomas that he was 'distressed to see its pernicious effect in your work because I believe you to be outstanding amongst your generation'. He finally agreed to publish *Twenty-five Poems*, although 'I cannot understand the meaning of the poems, but in this matter I have decided to put myself aside and let you and the public face each other.' Thomas, for his part, came to regard his publisher as 'a cliché-riddled hack'. Had he lived to read *Over the Bridge* he might have thought more kindly of his editor and fellow-poet.

JEREMY LEWIS is a freelance writer and editor. His biography of David Astor, the former editor/proprietor of the *Observer*, was published in March.

Collapse in the Colony

PATRICK WELLAND

With two prize-winning novels behind him – *Troubles* and *The Siege of Krishnapur* (see *SF* nos. 49 and 50) – J. G. Farrell felt sufficiently confident to paint his next exploration of the decline of the British Empire on a larger canvas. *The Singapore Grip* (1978), set in the build-up to Japan's invasion of the colony in 1942, continues the theme of its predecessors in portraying a complacent élite teetering on the edge of an abyss and then tumbling to its fate. But while the events of *Troubles* and *Siege* are experienced by a limited cast of protagonists in isolated circumstances – a decaying hotel in Ireland after the First World War and a besieged British Residency during the Indian Mutiny – those of *Grip* explore a more disparate society fracturing under stress.

At the book's heart are opposing notions about the exercise of power represented by the prosperous rubber trader and colonial diehard Walter Blackett and the idealistic son of Walter's business partner, Matthew Webb. However, as the menace of invasion draws closer, Farrell broadens his vision to incorporate exploited Chinese and Malay workers, incompetent military commanders and invading Japanese troops. He wanted to do more than write about the collapse of power. He wanted to penetrate the darkness that lay behind the acquisition of that power: the rapacity of imperial greed and its corrupting effects.

Farrell displayed impressive zeal himself in researching what his

J. G. Farrell, *The Singapore Grip* (1978)
Weidenfeld & Nicolson · Pb · 704pp · £9.99 · ISBN 9781857994926

biographer Lavinia Greacen calls his 'personal *War and Peace*'. He buried himself in the colony's commercial, social, political and military life between the wars and pinned a large-scale street map of Singapore over his desk. A bibliography – unusual for a work of fiction – lists fifty-one books from which he culled information. Later, he also visited Singapore and was struck by a powerful sensation of privilege surviving from earlier days.

As ever, Farrell's voice is ironic and his mischievously satirical observations on the absurdities of life are very funny. But unlike *Troubles* and *Siege*, which generally treat the main characters with what might be called critical sympathy, behind *Grip* lies a rage at the injustice wreaked by the strong on the weak. Again, Farrell was writing as modern events reflected his interpretation of the past. Just as *Troubles* had been written when British troops were surging into Ulster, so *Grip* was begun as the Americans retreated from Saigon. Again, Farrell was unsettled by the coincidence.

It is the late 1930s and Walter, the domineering head of the Singapore rubber-trading house of Blackett and Webb, examines the state of his affairs. At one level, all seems well. Profits are healthy and life in the wealthy suburb of Tanglin continues, with its familiar round of drinks at the Club, tennis matches and cocktail parties, the cogs discreetly oiled by servants. But the old colonial buccaneer, an almost feral presence the hairs on the ridge of whose back rise when he is roused by rage or lust, cannot avoid the feeling that his world is rapidly crumbling. The Japanese puppet government in Peking is freezing out foreign trade. For the past decade, strikes have been breaking out among his previously docile workforce. Are they really on our side or have those bloody communists got to them? As for Singapore, the old days when a chap could drive forty miles to dinner in his pyjamas and everybody knew everybody are gone. Then there are the children. Walter's brittle, flirtatious daughter Joan shows no sign of looking for a suitable husband, while his feckless son Monty seems more interested in drink and sex than the family business.

Following the death of old Mr Webb, the company founder – who in his dotage had taken to pruning his roses in the nude – his son Matthew arrives to join the firm. Walter is immediately alert to the possibilities of a match with Joan. She cynically agrees to seduce the young man with a view to cementing the family fortunes. But is Matthew really such a sound choice? The young fellow has eccentric notions about the equality of man from his time working at the League of Nations, and he seems to think that the lot of the work-force, uprooted from their homes and living in squalid tenements, could bear improvement. This is not the Blackett and Webb view at all, for the firm is founded on exploitation and its profits are main-tained by market rigging. Not that Walter would put it so bluntly. Recalling without shame how old Webb had once cheated Burmese peasants out of their land and turned them into dependent seasonal workers, he proudly declares that the early commercial pioneers 'armed only with a little capital and great creative vision, set the mark of civilization, bringing prosperity to themselves and . . . a means of livelihood to unhappy millions of Asiatics who had been faced by misery and destitution until their coming!'

Matthew, suspicious of such assumptions but aware of his own ignorance, fears instead that Malaya is 'a mere sweat shop for cheap labour operated in the interests of capitalism by cynical Western governments'. He believes in a fairer society for all. But his increasingly strident arguments are unheeded by a society fatally addicted to its own privileges. Walter is politely uncomprehending. Monty, selfish and insensitive, is mocking. Major Brendan Archer, last encountered in *Troubles* and now serving in Singapore, is fretfully aware that somehow the ruling clique has abused its power but he is too loyal to protest strongly.

Spurning Joan's attentions, Matthew forms a relationship with the Eurasian Vera Chiang who confirms his moral doubts by opening his eyes to the human price paid by the migrant hordes servicing the needs of Empire. She takes him to a Chinese 'dying house' where he is brought face to face with an old man, his health wrecked by work on the plantations, who describes how European inspectors cheated the rubber smallholders. Matthew is uncomfortably aware that through his stake in Blackett and Webb he is indirectly complicit in these excesses.

As Matthew worries about society and Walter about his rubber supplies, the feared Japanese assault becomes a reality. Again mingling fiction with historical fact, Farrell charts the devastating invasion of the Malayan peninsula through the eyes of the opposing armies. Young Private Kikuchi is fired by the Emperor's call to deliver 100 million Asians from the tyranny of 300,000 whites 'sucking their blood'. But even he, eager warrior that he is, is unsettled by the almost demonic Lieutenant Matsushita, 'an officer with strangely burning eyes' who is as happy to hurl himself into action, ignoring bullets raining down 'like a spring shower', as he is to kill poisonous snakes and eat their livers so as to strengthen his martial spirit.

In contrast to this unnerving zealotry, the Allied commanders Air Chief Marshal Sir Henry Robert Moore Brooke-Popham and Lieutenant-General Arthur Percival are plagued by agonies of indecision as defences once deemed invulnerable are swept aside. But Farrell is too clever to paint a caricature of bungling Blimps stumbling towards inevitable destruction. Instead, he quietly leads us to feel sympathy for these hapless relics from the First World War who are in charge of often untrained men armed with obsolete equipment, without naval or air support, and who watch with bewilderment the collapse of their plans.

Meanwhile civil disorder and inter-racial strife spread before the advancing Japanese, opening British eyes to the alarming realization that the native population over whom they have held sway for so long has no respect for a master now brought low. To the accompaniment of violence and rape, looters descend on abandoned European properties like a cloud of locusts, stripping them of everything of value.

With the first blackout, Singapore wakes to the prospect of immi-
nent horror: 'History had once more switched its points; this time
most abruptly to send them careering along a track which curved
away into a frightening darkness, beyond which lay their destina-
tion.' Soon, silver-winged bombers, 'slipping like fish through a
sluice-gate', unleash their cargo over the unprotected colony while
shells crash in from the advancing troops. Fighter planes fly low,
raking the panic-stricken streets with machine-gun fire. A once
ordered society is as comprehensively levelled as the blazing buildings
which crumple into rubble. Stoical as ever, Major Archer rises to
heroic heights as a firefighter; the docks are packed with fleeing
whites, Chinese, Malays and Indians; hierarchy is replaced by universal fear; demoralized troops drunkenly rampage out of control; roads
are choked with abandoned possessions; Matthew tries to flee with
his lover Vera but their boat is hijacked by Australian troops. To the
strong, the spoils. Just as self-interest built Singapore, so it accom-
panies its fall.

And Walter? Like Hitler denying reality in his bunker beneath the
ruins of Berlin, he holes up in his warehouse to watch over his rubber
supplies as the city burns about him. Even as he gazes from his
godown at the destruction of all that once seemed so secure, his old
instincts remain unquelled: 'Probably in a matter of months we'll
have to come to some understanding with Japan and everything will
continue as before. Except that in this case it won't happen as before
. . . Why? Because a lot of self-righteous bloody fools will have
destroyed our investments lock stock and barrel . . . and we shall have
to start again from scratch!'

The Singapore Grip is a long book whose wide compass renders it
less tightly controlled than *Troubles* and *Siege*, and it has been argued
that some of the passages dealing with historical facts intrude on the
narrative sweep. But they are never didactic and they add authority
to Farrell's indignant mission to expose the abuses by which empire
was created and sustained. And then, above all, there is the sheer

individuality of Farrell's prose and his extraordinary ability to leaven the seriousness of his message with a wry sense of humour.

Take, for example, Vera's attempt to educate Matthew in the complexities of Eastern sex, an infinitely more sacred process than the Western manner 'which to her resembled nothing so much as a pair of drunken rickshaw coolies colliding briefly at some foggy crossroads at dead of night'. After pointing out various important parts of the body (head of turtle, pearl on jade threshold, secret pouch), and touching on the Five Natural Moods, Five Revealing Signs, Hundred Anxious Feelings and Five Male Overstrainings, she

could now begin to explain what he would need to know to bring to a successful conclusion their first and relatively simple manoeuvre known as Bamboo Swaying in Spring Wind. After that, they might have a go at Butterfly Hovering over Snow Peony and then later . . . she might wake up a girlfriend . . . and invite her to join them in Goldfish Mouthing in Crystal Tank if they were not too tired. But for the moment Matthew still had a few things to learn.

Daniel Macklin

Poor Matthew's sexual ignorance includes the precise nature of the Singapore Grip itself, which he variously believes is a handshake, a tropical fever, a rattan suitcase and even a double-bladed hairpin. It is, in fact, a sexual technique employed by Singapore prostitutes. Finally enlightened just before he is marched off by the Japanese to Changi jail, he has his own definition: 'I know what it is! It's the grip of our Western culture and economy on the Far East . . . it's the stranglehold of capital . . . the doing of things our way . . . the pursuit of self-interest rather than of the common interest.' So Farrell believed – and reading *Grip* it is hard to disagree.

By the time of his death Farrell had completed in draft about half of a further Empire novel, set in Victorian Simla and posthumously published under the title *The Hill Station* (1981). It is sobering to think what this writer of unmatched originality could have gone on to achieve. But let us be grateful for his completed trilogy. As we move from the decaying hotel of *Troubles* to the besieged Residency in *The Siege of Krishnapur* and then to colonial collapse in *The Singapore Grip* we see Farrell's horizons and grand ambition expanding. In writing about people 'undergoing history' he examines the corrosive nature of power and cultural 'superiority', and the danger of settled ideas – dark themes still relevant today. But the overall tone is not so much pessimistic as compassionate. With a lightness of touch that belies the seriousness of his intent, Farrell charts our follies and perplexities with irony and laconic humour. Humans will always blunder. But there is ever hope of a better world.

PATRICK WELLAND is a former journalist caught in the Sussex Grip, in which victims stare at beautiful countryside for lengthy periods of time wondering what to do with the rest of their lives.

Ian Stephens, 'Thrush',
wood engraving

Love and Miss Lotti

SUE GEE

Was anyone ever as singular as Charlotte Mew? Mannish, gruffish, diminutive, she ranged about London in her tailor-mades and cropped hair and rolled her own cigarettes, possibly with the discarded drafts of poems. She gave mesmerizing readings and was published, alongside Henry James, in *The Yellow Book* in 1894, and in 1914 in *The Egoist* by Ezra Pound. Though sometimes awkward to the point of rudeness, she attracted devoted friends and admirers. A bright, funny child, hypersensitive to colour and atmosphere; a schoolgirl who had all her friends in fits; an accomplished pianist – yet Mew became the disturbing, sometimes harrowing poet of the outsider, the outcast, which was what she felt herself to be.

I first came across her in Mrs Roberts's Elocution class in 1964, where I learnt by heart her extraordinary poem of 1912, 'The Changeling'. Mrs Roberts urged 'Expression, dear' on us all; it wasn't hard to put it into lines like these:

> Toll no bell for me, dear Father, dear Mother,
> Waste no sighs.
> There are my sisters, there is my little brother,
> Who plays in the place called Paradise.
> Your children all, your children for ever,
> But I, so wild your disgrace, with the queer brown face,
> Was never never, I know, but half your child . . .

Penelope Fitzgerald, *Charlotte Mew and Her Friends* (1984)
Fourth Estate · Pb · 304pp · £10.99 · ISBN 9780007142743

What made Mew a 'disgrace', what tormented her, was the knowledge that she was made to love women, not men. Deeply divided between the strict moral code of her upbringing and her secret, sometimes overwhelming desires, she became in effect two people, ill at ease with both. To compound her suffering, when she did fall in love, as Penelope Fitzgerald reveals in *Charlotte Mew and Her Friends* (1984), 'she always chose wrong'.

None of this is ever explicit in her work. Instead, in her narrative poems, she gives voice to others who suffer from loneliness and longing, brought sometimes to breaking point. The changeling, smuggled by goblins into the nursery, is snatched away one wild wet night: 'All night long they danced in the rain,/Round and round in a dripping chain . . .' And the poem concludes bleakly: 'I shall grow up, but never grow old/I shall always, always be very cold,/I shall never come back again.'

Charlotte Mew – 'Lotti' in the nursery, 'Miss Lotti' as she grew up – was born in 1869, the second child of an architect, Fred Mew, who came to London from the Isle of Wight at the age of 14 and, like Thomas Hardy, learned his trade on the job. He married the daughter of his employer, and the difference in their social standing would always be a part of the family's consciousness: after his death, when money was a struggle, Charlotte sought to provide her monstrously demanding mother with 'a good address'.

The nursery at the top of the first family house, in Bloomsbury, was haunted by 'the remorseless punctual infant mortality' of the Victorian age. Three children died, two as babies, and Charlotte never forgot the little pale brother who makes an appearance in 'The Changeling': Richard, who had scarlet fever at the age of 5, and whom she was brought to see in death. Four children remained, ruled by the powerful housekeeper/nurse/governess Elizabeth Goodman. 'To us children,' Charlotte wrote, 'she was as fixed a part of the universe as the bath.'

Elizabeth was loving, but full of Judgement Day, and her dire biblical warnings created in curly, brilliant, irresistible and defiant Lotti a cast of mind in which she knew she was guilty. Though Charlotte later described her childhood as magical, there is no doubt that this sense of guilt was to contribute hugely to her later melancholia and the unending struggle to keep her true nature hidden. 'Guilt of this nature can never be eradicated,' writes Fitzgerald; 'a lifetime is not enough.'

Her adored older brother Henry and brilliant little Freda were both to succumb in adolescence to schizophrenia. Both were committed to asylums, and the need to support them there was a lifelong financial anxiety for Charlotte and the younger Anne. Five children had effectively become two, and if there was anyone whom Charlotte loved truly, deeply and devotedly all her life, it was the gentle, artistic little sister, with whom, together with 'Ma' and a malevolent parrot called Wek, she was to live until all were gone. What followed then was tragedy.

A 'reading and writing child', in 1879 she began attending Gower Street School, presided over by Miss Lucy Harrison. This clever, inspiring young woman was to become Charlotte's first, passionate love; when she heard that Miss Harrison had suddenly left, ill through overwork, she sprang up from the piano and, remembered a fellow-pupil, 'in a wild state of grief began to bang her head against the wall'. It was, Fitzgerald notes, 'the end of Lotti's schooling, and part of her education had been to know what it was to be totally obsessed with the physical presence or absence of another woman . . . it proved to be an initiation into life's pattern'.

Two more such passions were to overwhelm her. The first was for Ella D'Arcy, assistant editor of *The Yellow Book*, another clever and distinctive woman – though, unlike Lucy Harrison, she was unequivocally interested in men. 'A mouse-mannered piece of sex' was how an enemy described her. When she left, in 1902, Charlotte followed her to Paris and, finding her living in one-room poverty, did her best to help her, taking on teatime visits 'the little necessaries for the occasion – flowers, cakes, etc.' She was in a state of enchanted excitement, but 'How much did Ella care, or even notice?'

Charlotte returned to London feeling as though she had been spat upon, and some of the verses she wrote then are keyed up to hysterical pitch. But then came this measured, sombre epitaph on that mad dash for love.

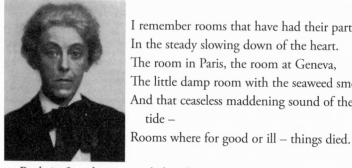

> I remember rooms that have had their part
> In the steady slowing down of the heart.
> The room in Paris, the room at Geneva,
> The little damp room with the seaweed smell
> And that ceaseless maddening sound of the
> tide –
> Rooms where for good or ill – things died.

Back in London, overwhelmed with domestic duties, she tried feature-writing and had a long essay on Emily Brontë's poetry accepted by *Temple Bar*, a magazine to which she became a regular contributor. It folded in 1905 and for the next three years she seems to have had almost no new work published. Things changed when in 1912 *The Nation* took a remarkable poem, 'The Farmer's Bride', in which a lonely farmer mourns the terrified frigidity of his young wife. There are shades of Hardy in its rural voice and setting, and its marvellous shifts of rhythm, but it marked her out as strong and original. With these six verses Charlotte for the first time attracted notice and respect as a poet.

She was immediately taken up by Amy Dawson Scott – the founder of International PEN. Dawson Scott invited her to give salon readings and introduced her to the woman with whom Charlotte was, for the last time, to fall helplessly in love. This was the novelist, suffragette and follower of Freud and Jung, the indefatigable May Sinclair. For a long time their friendship was close. May did much to introduce Charlotte's work to the London avant-garde of Wyndham

Lewis and Ezra Pound, and Charlotte was grateful. But it was more than gratitude, and in 1914 she made a humiliating pass which May later laughed about in public. Nothing could have been more coruscatingly painful, and between 1914 and 1918, the war years, Charlotte wrote a group of poems about shameful exposures and betrayal. At least one of these, 'Saturday Market', in which a wretched woman conceals from jeering onlookers a baby – 'a dead red thing' – beneath a ragged shawl, is devastating.

But happily, during these years she found just the right place to welcome and admire her. 'Are you Charlotte Mew?' she was asked on her first, invited visit to the Poetry Bookshop. Charlotte, emerging from the evening fog like a tiny maiden aunt, gave a slight smile. 'I'm sorry to say that I am.'

The bookshop, located in a squalid bit of Bloomsbury, 'full of small workshops, dustbins and cats', was presided over by Harold Monro, a man with a private income who was 'determined to do something about poetry'. In a shop with a small coal fire and a table laden with books, he published on a shoestring, sold poetry and gave sanctuary. He knew people. He and his assistant Alida, a beautiful young Polish woman, adored one another and, although he was homosexual, eventually married. It was Alida who organized the weekly readings at which Charlotte began to shine.

Monro published her first collection, *Saturday Market*, in 1916, just before he was called up. Alida sent it to Sydney Cockerell, the influential and energetic director of the Fitzwilliam Museum in Cambridge. And with his enthusiastic reception of this book, everything began to change. Charlotte suddenly had a friend who took her under his wing and introduced her to many, including his invalid wife, the artist Kate Cockerell, with whom a real friendship developed. He introduced her to Hardy, who pronounced her 'far and away the best living woman poet . . . who will be read when others are forgotten'. Best of all, at a moment when the Mews, faced with the end of the lease on their dilapidated house, moved to upper-floor rooms in Camden Town, Cockerell got her a Civil List pension.

Relieved at last from money worries, Charlotte in 1924 and 1925 had perhaps the happiest years of her life. But all this time the great constant had been the gentle love, admiration and encouragement of her little sister. Their mother, at the end 'a tiny bag of bones', had died in 1922. In the autumn of 1926, Anne fell seriously ill. A change of air – they took rooms in Chichester – did no good. She died the following year, and with her death Charlotte began to unravel.

In danger of passing from the neurotic to the psychotic, she refused to enter an asylum but was persuaded by her doctor to go to the gloomiest of nursing homes, near Baker Street station. 'There is', writes Fitzgerald, 'something inexplicable in the choice of this place.' And here, in the spring of 1928, she drank a bottle of Lysol and ended her gifted, tortured life. It was, Cockerell wrote in his diary, 'a tragic end to the tragic life of a very rare being'.

Fitzgerald's sympathy for Charlotte Mew is profound, her understanding complete. The Poetry Bookshop was a haunt of her own childhood, when the rhyme sheets Monro had printed (and which Charlotte and Anne both coloured) were pinned on her nursery walls. 'A whole generation of children learned to love poetry from these rhyme sheets,' she writes, and she was one of them.

Her Life is full of light, razor-sharp insights, literary and personal, with acute remarks about what it means to be a writer. It is this sensitive identification, and the gentle humour which inflects all her work, which turns what could be a deeply saddening life story into something both moving and uplifting, as one woman writer shows us the struggles and gifts of another.

SUE GEE still has 'The Changeling' by heart, and introduced it into her novel, *Coming Home*, in which a lonely boy feels it is speaking just to him.

Hero Ahead of His Time

URSULA BUCHAN

I spent the freezing cold winter of 1976 working in a flowering bulb nursery in Haarlem in Holland. Every day after work, I slipped and slid along frozen canals on wooden skates that Pieter Bruegel would have recognized, then retired to my room to try to teach myself Dutch. I was young and sometimes homesick, so I turned quite often in relief to English books that I borrowed from the local library. One day I found a copy of *Montrose*, written by my grandfather, John Buchan, and published in 1928. Despite having been taught at university to be pretty sniffy about any history that made personality, rather than socio-economic forces, the driver of great events, I nevertheless thankfully abandoned my Dutch and read the book straight through.

I wrote to my 93-year-old grandmother to tell her how much I had been moved, impressed and, frankly, horrified by it. She replied that she was very pleased that I had come to discover the merits of *Montrose* for myself, since she had made a point of never pressing her husband's works upon the grandchildren he had died too early to meet.

This was the perfect truth, which even now makes me want to cry out: 'Why ever not?' Was it an habitual reticence, in a woman who was 19 when Queen Victoria died, or a fear that I might be put off

---

John Buchan's *Montrose* (1928) and *Witch Wood* (1927) are both out of print. However, copies are available from second-hand booksellers, in particular SMS Books of Loughborough (peter.thackeray@ntlworld.com), a proportion of whose profits go to help support the John Buchan Museum in Peebles.

the man and his hundred books by pressure from her, or even, perhaps, an unassuaged grief, that struck her dumb and denied me the
priceless knowledge of how and why and in what way the books were
written? I can recall us talking of the works of writers she had known
– H. G. Wells, A. L. Rowse, Virginia Woolf and Henry Newbolt – as
well as of the German poets she liked, especially Goethe and Heine,
but rarely, if ever, of her husband's books. So, although I have read
and reread his twenty-eight novels over the years – especially when I'm
ill or out of sorts, and in need of sprightly prose and gripping excitement – it's taken me half a lifetime to discover and take pleasure in
the short stories, the poetry (much of it in Scots dialect), the military
histories, the political thought and, of course, the biographies – of
Oliver Cromwell, Sir Walter Raleigh, Augustus, Julius Caesar, Sir
Walter Scott, as well as the Marquis of Montrose. It's been my loss.

In the 1920s, Buchan wrote his fiction and non-fiction at week-
ends at his home near Oxford, after busy weeks spent in London
working for the publisher Thomas Nelson, as well as Reuters and,
from 1927, as a Conservative MP. *Montrose* was the fruit of much
research in contemporary accounts and pamphlets (he had a well-
stocked library) and indeed was a second stab at the subject. In 1913,
he had published a shorter book, mainly dealing with Montrose's
campaigns, but he had not yet learned to be entirely objective about
his hero and the result was not popular with the critics.

He made a much better fist of the task the second time round. He
said his aim was to 'present a great figure in its appropriate setting'
and for someone like me, brought up in England and completely
ignorant of the religious struggles in seventeenth-century Scotland,
this is exactly what he does. This book may one day be superseded in
scholarship (although apparently it is still considered the definitive
biography) but I should be surprised if it were ever bettered for read-
ability. Clarity of thought, brevity of expression, acute historical
imagination, breadth of learning and courage of conviction were the
hallmarks of his biographies, and *Montrose* exhibits all these qualities.

His subject, James Graham (1612–50), head of the clan Graham, was certainly a remarkable man. Scholar, sportsman and poet, he was a devout Presbyterian who signed the National Covenant against the imposition of Laud's prayer book in 1638 and opposed Charles I, before coming to realize that the Covenanters were determined to extend their influence into the civil sphere and establish an oppressive theocracy. This he could not support, which is why he never signed the Solemn League and Covenant of 1643, the promise made by Scottish Presbyterians to join with English Parliamentarians against the King.

During what is now known as the War of the Three Kingdoms, Charles made him a Marquess and then, in 1645, his Captain-General in Scotland, although initially he had no army. He travelled from Carlisle to Scotland disguised as a groom, with 'two followers, four sorry horses, little money and no baggage'. However, he was joined by the Earl of Antrim's 2,000 well-trained Irish levies, under the charismatic leadership of Alasdair Macdonald, known as 'Colkitto', and together they won a series of stunning military encounters for the King, often when seriously outnumbered. The most notable were Tippermuir in 1644, and Inverlochy, Auldearn, Alford and Kilsyth in 1645.

All Scotland was now at Montrose's feet but, after Charles's defeat at Naseby, it could not last. In the end, Montrose was beaten by the treachery, self-interest or half-heartedness of Scottish chieftains, Colkitto's defection to wage his own battle against the Marquess of Argyll and clan Campbell, and the brilliance of another great commander, David Leslie, who caught Montrose by surprise at Philiphaugh in the Borders in September 1645, and ruined the Royalist cause in Scotland until the return of Charles II. It is hard to hold back the tears when reading the account of Montrose's betrayal, capture, removal to Edinburgh and brave death by hanging, aged only 37, in 1650.

The strengths of *Montrose* are the vivid descriptions of weather and

landscape, the understanding of military tactics, religious profund-
ities and political wranglings, and the portrayal of a man (usually)
of honour and integrity, a romantic who was cast in a heroic mould
and born well ahead of his time.

Montrose won the James Tait Black Memorial Prize, but I should
be surprised if it is on many people's reading list these days. Modern
books about the man apparently tend to concentrate on his military
exploits, which were impressive, but the religion and politics, especially the reasons why Montrose, a good Presbyterian, rejected the
Solemn Covenant, seem to me to be as important. Montrose was
committed to religious toleration, at a time when that was widely
considered the Devil's work in Scotland. That, for Buchan, was his
crowning glory. Not everyone will agree with the author's conclu-
sions, but the argument is well made. And his belief that individual
personalities change history is now back in fashion, with even such a
respected historian as Margaret MacMillan writing a book entitled
History's People.

Buchan believed that *Witch Wood* (1927), the novel he wrote at the
same time and which drew on the sources he studied for *Montrose*,
was his best work of historical fiction; and many commentators since
have agreed. In it, Montrose plays a crucial, if mostly off-stage part,
winning over the earnest, ardent and scholarly young minister of the
Kirk, David Sempill, who has the cure of souls in a benighted parish
in Tweeddale, called Woodilee. Woodilee was based on Broughton,
where Buchan's mother was brought up, on the edge of the ancient
Wood of Caledon.

Some of the self-righteous Calvinists in his congregation, who
believe that their 'Elect' status entitles them to do whatever they like,
are practising witchcraft in the wood; David, with the help of a lovely
young gentlewoman, Katrine Yester, with whom he falls in love, as
well as a few villagers of generally ill-repute, determines to root it out.
In the process, he uncovers hypocrisy and licentiousness on a grand
scale, but he brings down the wrath of his blinkered Kirk superiors,

haters of the 'malignant' Montrose and deeply suspicious of Sempill's emphasis on Christian charity to all.

Buchan took more care over this book, particularly the psychology and the characterization, than over his rollicking adventure stories, and devised some memorable characters, such as David's friend and Montrose's captain, Mark Kerr, whose denunciation of fundamentalist Bible literalism is a *tour de force* and accurately describes Buchan's own attitude to the Calvinistic tradition in which he was bred. Sempill is one of Buchan's most cherished character types: the scholar called to action. He is also one of the most complex. This is a book of light and shade, of paradisaical contentment and stark tragedy, and it stays with you.

Much of the dialogue is in Borders dialect, which was already in rapid retreat by the 1920s and has now all but disappeared, so the modern reader may need to call up an online dictionary of Scottish words (I suggest www.dsl.ac.uk). But you get used to Lowland Scots surprisingly quickly and it's an idiom that adds mightily to the power of the language – as does the author's sure use of biblical texts, learned as a boy during long Sabbath services. Those readers who don't want to take on a detailed, lengthy biography will be pleased to know that there is probably enough sound history in *Witch Wood* to satisfy them.

Both *Montrose* and *Witch Wood* are compelling expositions of the disastrous consequences of religious fanaticism: destructive both to society and to the faith it perverts. This is something that resonates like a clanging bell with us today. It is possible to draw a pretty straight line between the Scottish Covenanters of the mid-seventeenth century and the extreme Islamists of today. For that reason alone, if for no other, these books should still reward the thoughtful reader, more than eighty years after they were written.

URSULA BUCHAN is very glad not to have lived through the Civil War, but is happy to read about it from a safe distance. She is writing a biography of John Buchan for Bloomsbury.

Goodbye to All What?

VICTORIA NEUMARK

Lately I've been rereading books that impressed me in my youth. Some still impress, some no longer do, and some raise questions I would never have thought to ask when I took everything I read as simple truth. Now I find myself asking: what was Robert Graves saying 'goodbye' to? When he published *Goodbye to All That* (1929), his startling memoir of his youth and his experiences on the Western Front in the First World War, he was 34. Most of the book recalls events that had ended a decade earlier. He says: 'I had, by the age of 23, been born, initiated into a formal religion, travelled, learned to lie, loved unhappily, been married, gone to the war, taken life, procreated my kind, rejected formal religion, won fame and been killed.' Are these life events to which one can bid adieu?

Graves's bestseller broke fresh ground and turned the genre of the war memoir (previously the province of glory-hunting military men) on its head. He told how the daily terror of extinction, amid incessant noise and mud and dysentery, ground personal existence down to intensely vivid and interminably dull moments. In matter-of-fact prose, hardly altered from diaries and letters, Graves's stiff upper lip scarcely trembles. Even when severely wounded and near death at the Battle of Mametz Wood – when Graves believed he had actually died and been jolted back to life by the extreme pain of the ambulance journey – he does not weep and wail. This restraint gives the book an enduring – and endearing – solidity. As the poet Wilfred Owen

Robert Graves, *Goodbye to All That* (1929)
Penguin · Pb · 288pp · £8.99 · ISBN 9780141184593

famously wrote, 'My subject is War, and the pity of War. The poetry is in the pity.'

Incidents are described with hellish clarity. After the Battle of Loos, the clear-up party finds a dead officer who, only a few hours before, had been an inspiring leader. With seventeen wounds, he had died with his fist crammed into his mouth to stop himself crying out and attracting the attention of the enemy, having first sent a message apologizing for groaning. As such scenes unfold, the relentless recurrence of death deadens the living. Months later, Graves goes for a stroll and finds the bloated, stinking corpse of a German soldier, eyeglasses still on nose. He is upset, not by the sight, but because he realizes there is 'no excitement left . . . no horror in the experience of death'.

Graves is possibly the first writer to record how boredom as much as heroism forces men into crazy heroics. That, and the vileness of the trenches. At first the trenches were a novelty, so that people put up

J. Weston Lewis

with paddling about in water. But, as the years wore on, disgust overwhelmed soldiers. Sewage, rotting body parts and belligerent rats were ever-present companions.

Despite the battering of enemy fire, the dehumanizing filth and the widespread lack of faith in the war itself, men could still display their better natures. Some of the book's most poignant scenes tell of such step-changes: a Welsh fusilier playing a hand harp when the shelling pauses, a kindly adjutant finding two unripe greengages for the wounded Graves. In this way, the book is by no means an artless account of events unfolding but a closely shaped narrative.

War experiences form only the middle section of Graves's story, which is told in three parts. The first covers his childhood and youth, coloured and contoured by the rigid class distinctions of late Victorian and Edwardian England. And the final third takes up the story after the war, his marriage and efforts to make sense of civilian life, with an epilogue to the poet Laura Riding, added to a revised edition published in 1957.

His father, an inspector of schools who struggled in the shadow of a long line of Anglo-Irish bishops, was also a poet and songwriter of distinction. He wrote a popular hit called 'Father O'Flynn', of which Graves mordantly remarks that he 'sold the complete rights for a guinea. The publisher made thousands.' Robert's mother, who came from a long-established Bavarian family, had married his widowed father to help with five motherless children and went on to bear him five more. She was a softer but more insistent presence, instilling in her children an intense Protestant religiosity, a deep prudishness and a fear of sin.

Theirs was a Victorian household, with funds stretched to keep up appearances, so that the children were pushed to win scholarships. Bitterly, Graves observes that his inability to conjugate irregular Greek verbs dictated his going to Charterhouse rather than Winchester, since Charterhouse did not demand Greek. Though he does acknowledge his parents' generosity (they bailed him out repeatedly until his late twenties), this first part of the book is shot through with resentment. 'I paid so heavily for the 14 years of my gentleman's education,' he says.

How he paid is painfully spelled out. Forced to do mental arithmetic at the age of 6, he wet himself. At 7, he was removed from one prep school for using 'naughty words', which he understood as little as the Latin he was forced to recite. As he got older, he says, his character became fixed: 'I began playing games seriously, was quarrelsome, boastful and talkative, won prizes and collected things.' It's a sharp-eyed character sketch; yet Graves does not question, as I did in my rereading, why childhood injustices sting more sharply than war wounds in his memory. What does this say about the class system which is still so entrenched in British life? We haven't said goodbye to that, either.

Boys and masters at his schools were mostly insensitive and overbearing. He was beaten and his romantic but entirely non-sexual friendships were interpreted as 'beastliness'; his poetry was mocked as 'filthy'; and education was reduced to mechanical exercises, largely in Latin and Greek grammar. His salvation came when he discovered a talent for boxing, winning respect as well as a savage satisfaction. And he was introduced to climbing by one of the young masters, George Mallory, who was to die on his third attempt to climb Mount Everest.

Graves brings this vanished world to life, the backdrop to his decision to join up in 1914 – to avoid the grind of reading classics at Oxford, he claims. But really, as his near-contemporary Rupert Brooke was to suggest, the war seemed to all these young men, torn between the harsh and simple pieties with which their education had imbued them and their yearning for a 'cleaner' world, an answer and an escape at one fell swoop. It was not, of course, the sort of show such very young men imagined – over by Christmas and full of fine deeds – and yet so few rebelled. At least one in three of Graves's contemporaries at Charterhouse were killed. Even the poet Siegfried Sassoon, with whom Graves had a passionate, antagonistic friendship during the war and after, refused to avoid fighting, although he had condemned the war in an open letter to *The Times*. Overall, nearly 20 per cent of the officer class were killed in action, compared to 12 per cent of ordinary soldiers. As Owen wrote, they died for their belief in 'The old Lie: *Dulce et decorum est / Pro patria mori.*'

In these first two sections, Graves's voice rings true. He explains how the war changed him, as it did many others, from a self-confessed snob into a socialist. During his first command, he winced at the miners' coarse language and despaired at their limited horizons and sexual frankness. Yet these feelings wore away in the shared experiences of battle.

The third section of the book tells a less sympathetic story. His first wife, Nancy, sister of the painter Ben Nicholson, was an ardent feminist, who nearly refused to marry him when she discovered that the wedding service still contained the bride's promise to 'obey'. Thereafter, despite having four children, the couple were often at odds: Nancy needed her own life as an artist and illustrator; they disagreed over childcare; they failed to earn money in any of their ill-thought-out schemes, which included running a village shop and a school; and they relied on a steady drip-drip of 'loans' from Graves's parents to keep up their bohemian lifestyle. Graves attempted to complete his Oxford degree in the normal way but could not take the routine.

He describes 1918–26 as a period of gradual disintegration. While he achieved his first success as a writer with his biography of his friend T. E. Lawrence, his marriage was foundering. Although the couple had vowed that he need never get a job, he felt forced by poverty and by Nancy's ill-health to accept a handsome salary as Professor of English Literature at the newly founded Royal Egyptian University in Cairo. And here the story takes its strangest turn.

On a whim, Graves wrote to the young American poet Laura Riding, whose work had impressed him. She turned up at the docks, accompanied the family to Egypt and back again, became part of a *ménage à trois* – and then dispossessed Nancy. Graves glosses over these events. He ends the book claiming to have 'learned to tell the truth – mainly'; but by this time his words feel decidedly slippery.

Graves spent the years 1929–40 with Laura Riding, to whom he addresses his epilogue, describing her there as having the 'true quality of one living invisibly, against kind, as dead, beyond event' – a mind-boggling and somewhat mystifying claim. It was a fraught relationship, during the course of which, in a fit of jealousy, Laura threw herself out of a fourth-floor window. Graves ran downstairs, but was unable to reach her in time, and threw himself out of a third-floor window after her. Both survived, but Laura sustained spinal injuries while Graves got away with bruises.

'After which . . .' Graves elliptically concludes. After which, in fact, he earned a good living and fame while Riding, to her fury, faded into obscurity. Graves was grateful to her for shutting the door on the nightmares of his past, but I closed the book reflecting that the nightmares of our past are not so quickly dismissed. As Faulkner wrote in *Requiem for a Nun*, 'The past is never dead. It's not even past.' Wars are not done with, even now in Europe. Graves's tremendous account reminds us that we have said goodbye to none of that.

VICTORIA NEUMARK has spent more of her life than seems feasible reading, but only recently bought into the joys of rereading. As well as Robert Graves, she can recommend *In the Night Kitchen* and *The Very Hungry Crocodile*, which she is enjoying with her young granddaughter.

Ian Stephens, 'Robin',
wood engraving

Mostly in the Mind

DEREK COLLETT

I watched a lot of television in my twenties and I doubt whether it did me much good. But it did lead, indirectly, to my discovering the fascinating novels of Nigel Balchin.

In 1990 I saw a TV drama series, bought a copy of the book on which it had been based and, among the endpapers, spotted a notice for another novel that sounded intriguing: *The Small Back Room* by Nigel Balchin. I'd never heard of Balchin but tracked down *The Small Back Room*, read it and instantly became an ardent fan. I devoted much of the rest of the decade to finding and reading his other novels (he wrote fourteen in all), and now consider *Mine Own Executioner* to be one of the very best of them.

Balchin graduated from Cambridge in 1930 with a degree in Natural Sciences. He had studied psychology during his final term, and this enabled him to obtain a position as an industrial psychologist. In 1933, while on secondment to the confectioners Rowntree's, he helped the company launch a new chocolate assortment. How many people who put a box of Black Magic in their supermarket trolley today know that its colour scheme was the work of a famous novelist? Standing in front of a confectioner's shop window in search of inspiration, Balchin said that he could see every colour but black and realized that a black box would be both eye-catching and clearly differentiated from the competition, which relied in the early 1930s on classic staples of 'chocolate-box art' – ivy-clad cottages, rosy-cheeked children and adorable kittens and puppies.

Nigel Balchin, *Mine Own Executioner* (1945), is out of print.

During the early part of the Second World War, Balchin worked for the Ministry of Food, where he was responsible for the allocation of supplies of raw materials to chocolate manufacturers. This phase of his wartime career provided much of the material for his first well-received novel, *Darkness Falls from the Air* (1942). Then in 1941 he swopped butter for guns and joined the army. He helped to overhaul the service's personnel selection procedure before transferring to the army's scientific research wing, where he was responsible – among other things – for advising on the practicality of new weapons. His war work during this period informed *The Small Back Room* (1943: see *SF* no. 24). In 1945 he was promoted to Deputy Scientific Adviser to the Army Council and made a Brigadier at the age of just 36.

Balchin's attempts before the war to succeed as a writer had ended in failure. After a false start as a playwright, he wrote seven books in the mid-1930s but most of them sank without trace. It was not until the war had been in progress for more than three years that he wrote a successful novel. Lauded retrospectively as 'the classic novel of the London Blitz', *Darkness Falls from the Air* can be considered the point at which his writing career really took off. All 5,000 copies of the book – paper rationing prohibited a longer print run – sold in a trice.

The Small Back Room, which followed *Darkness Falls from the Air*, sold hundreds of thousands of copies and remains Balchin's finest achievement as a novelist. But his next book, *Mine Own Executioner* (1945), ran it very close in terms of sales, and a number of reviewers in the 1940s preferred it. L. P. Hartley called it 'a triumphant success – the kind of success that makes one want to clap', and John Betjeman characterized it as 'an exceptionally good novel'. Much more recently, Philippa Gregory has observed that *Mine Own Executioner* represents 'the most extraordinary exploration of the human condition'.

The novel tells the story of Felix Milne, a London psychoanalyst who divides his working life between his own private practice and a clinic offering free psychotherapy to those unable to pay for it. Balchin packs a lot of varied material into the first half of the novel.

The accounts of Milne's patients and their neuroses are fascinating, and the depiction of the psychoanalyst's strained relationship with his long-suffering wife Patricia is well observed and touching. If the scenes in which Milne attempts to start an affair with Patricia's best friend Barbara are less successful, they do at least furnish the book with an extra dimension.

The second half of *Mine Own Executioner* is very different. Having presented these various plot strands, Balchin picks out one of them and chooses to develop it more fully than the others. Adam Lucian is a young Spitfire pilot. Shot down over Burma during the war and captured by the Japanese, he manages to escape but then, back in London in peacetime, he attempts to strangle his wife Molly and so she persuades him to undergo analysis with Milne.

Milne injects Lucian with a hypnotic drug and coaxes his war memories out of him. Lucian reveals that he had given information to the Japanese under torture and Milne believes that it is this moment of self-perceived weakness (Lucian refers to his capitulation as 'a bloody disgraceful business') that has caused his patient to become mentally unbalanced. But is there more to it than that? Is there something buried in Lucian's subconscious that represents the real reason for the man's murderous designs on his wife? The rest of the book describes Milne's attempt to delve deeper into Lucian's mind before he harms Molly again.

There is much to enjoy in *Mine Own Executioner*. The principal players in the story are all likeable and interesting but the care Balchin lavishes on his minor characters – a consistent strength of his fiction – is arguably even more impressive. Several of Milne's patients lodge in the memory and Balchin also draws superb pen portraits of the psychoanalyst's colleagues at the clinic: 'Tautz, about five feet two and completely round, Phyllis Snow, a school-teacher with a secret sorrow, and Paston . . . looking like a commercial traveller for something rather shady'. There is a very amusing description of a cocktail party and in the book's penultimate chapter we are treated to what must surely be one of the most entertaining courtroom scenes in twentieth-century fiction.

The book is not perfect by any means. Balchin usually excelled at penning fresh, lively dialogue but some of the language in this novel grates on the modern ear. (When he reviewed the book in 1945, Peter Quennell remarked that Balchin possessed 'a knack of writing dialogue (intended, I suppose, to be smartly topical) which causes the gorge to rise and sets the teeth on edge'.) He also struggled throughout most of his career to create believable female characters and, true to form, Patricia and Barbara are not as convincingly drawn as the male characters in the book.

Mine Own Executioner was filmed in 1947 in an agreeably noirish way, the script being written by Balchin himself. It may seem a little stiff and wordy to the contemporary viewer but, with its exciting, thriller-style ending, it still stands up as one of the better British films of the late 1940s and one of the best screen representations of psychoanalysis.

Balchin was not a psychoanalyst, however, so where did he obtain his material? I believe that most of it came from speaking to the psychiatrists with whom he had worked during his wartime stint as a member of the army's personnel selection unit. As Balchin said himself, the psychoanalytical content of *Mine Own Executioner* 'was based more on my experience of psychiatry during the war than on anything I learnt at Cambridge'.

When he had finished writing the novel, Balchin was dissatisfied with it, largely because he felt he had allowed the plot to run away with itself and smother the psychoanalytical theme in the process. He tried to tear up the manuscript, failed and instead just hurled the (unnumbered) pages in the air in fury. His wife came into his study and said 'I see exactly how you feel but I don't think I'd just throw it away.' The many readers who have derived pleasure from reading the novel over the last seventy years owe Elisabeth Balchin a debt of gratitude for persuading her husband to persevere with it.

Almost as soon as the accolades that Balchin received for writing *Mine Own Executioner* had died away, the author's troubled personal life began to affect his writing career. An initially light-hearted partner-swopping arrangement with the artist Michael Ayrton ended when Elisabeth fell irreversibly in love with him. Balchin divorced her in 1951 and she married Ayrton the following year. Life for Balchin was never quite the same again without Elisabeth. He remarried in 1953, his new bride being his young Yugoslav secretary Yovanka Tomich, but his second marriage was a turbulent one, undermined by his increasing dependence on alcohol. He drank very heavily from the late 1940s onwards and ended up an alcoholic.

Balchin died in 1970, aged 61. He has been largely forgotten by the literary world over the intervening thirty-five years but some writers still admire him: Clive James for one has observed that Balchin was 'in many ways the missing writer of the Forties'. Because he wrote with a psychologist's sure grip about universal concerns – life and death, love and loss, right and wrong – Balchin's novels have a timeless quality. *Mine Own Executioner, Darkness Falls from the Air, The Small Back Room* and a handful of others are also immensely readable and deserve a place on the bookshelves of all bibliophiles.

Ten years in the making, DEREK COLLETT's biography of Balchin, *His Own Executioner: The Life of Nigel Balchin*, was published last year.

Letters from the Heart

DAISY HAY

Over the past few months I've been immersed in a feast of late-eighteenth-century reading as I've meandered through the foothills of a new book project. I've had the delight of reacquainting myself with old friends and have made some new ones along the way as I've lived and breathed the turbulent events of the decade following the French Revolution through the eyes of some of the period's most brilliant writers.

One rediscovery has stood out. Mary Wollstonecraft's *Letters Written in Sweden, Norway and Denmark* was widely praised when it was first published in 1796. Wollstonecraft's husband William Godwin described it as a book 'calculated to make a man in love with its author' and several of his contemporaries agreed. Wordsworth and Coleridge were both influenced by its descriptions of the natural world, and even usually censorious reviewers reacted with enthusiasm. A magazine called the *British Critic* thought it the work of a woman 'exquisitely alive to the beauties of nature, and keenly susceptible of every soft impression, every tender emotion', and the *Monthly Review* wrote that it was characterized by 'the natural and energetic expression of feelings which do credit to the writer's heart'.

Yet *Letters Written in Sweden* is little read nowadays outside academic circles. My rereading of it has convinced me that it is ripe for a revival, not least because it speaks to many of the things that preoccupy us today. The topics covered in this odd, hybrid book include

Mary Wollstonecraft, *Letters Written in Sweden, Norway and Denmark* (1796)
OUP · Pb · 240pp · £8.99 · ISBN 9780199230631

all the things you might expect to find in a work of travel writing: descriptions of foreign climates, landscapes and customs, a smattering of history, more than a smattering of politics, and reflections on the country left behind. But this is a work which also takes in parenting, a hopeless love affair and a journey of self-discovery and restoration. It may be over two hundred years old but it was written when Europe was in flux and it feels to me like a book for our own uncertain times, with much to say about the way in which the act of writing can remake us.

An unlikely constellation of events led Mary Wollstonecraft to compose the *Letters*. By the mid-1790s she had made her name as a writer, having published her famous *Vindication of the Rights of Woman* as well as a host of lesser-known works. In 1792, shortly after *Vindication* appeared, she travelled to Paris to witness the French Revolution at first hand and there she met an American businessman called Gilbert Imlay. As the Revolution descended into violent chaos, Wollstonecraft and Imlay embarked on an affair and in 1794 Wollstonecraft gave birth to a baby girl whom she named Fanny. For a brief period she was able to dream of a happy future in which she, Imlay and Fanny would live together in domestic bliss. But Imlay had other ideas, and his absences from Wollstonecraft's fireside grew longer and more frequent.

In 1795 she packed up her life in France and returned to England with Fanny, only to find that Imlay had no intention of making a home with her there. In desperation she took an overdose of laudanum, scaring Imlay out of indecisive prevarication and into action. His solution was not that she and Fanny should live with him, but that they should travel on his behalf to Scandinavia to enquire into the fate of a ship he had chartered. Like many other speculators of the period Imlay was attempting to profit from the French Revolution in ways that were barely legal, and in a complicated set of transactions he had arranged for a cargo of silver to be sent to Gothenburg. The ship disappeared en route and Imlay suspected foul play on the

Anna Trench

part of the captain. So he dispatched Wollstonecraft north to find the ship and to win his cargo of silver back for him.

It was an audacious way to treat the lover he had spurned, and very few women of the period would have accepted such a task, especially with a toddler in tow. But Wollstonecraft was not like other women and in June 1795 she set sail from Hull with Fanny and a French nursemaid at her side. For several months she travelled through Sweden, Norway and Denmark, writing letters to Imlay along the way. She discovered that Imlay's suspicions about the ship's captain were correct but, faced with considerable hostility from an impenetrable foreign legal system, she was unable to secure the return of his silver. When she got back to London she discovered that he was living openly with another woman and she made a second attempt at suicide, throwing herself into the Thames at Putney Bridge. Again she survived, and as she recovered she began to realize that she must make a life for herself and Fanny in which Imlay played no part. She demanded her letters back and in the final months of 1795 reworked them into a book, removing some of the most personal sections but otherwise leaving much of the pain of the originals as a public testament to her suffering. The result was a work quite unlike other travel books of the period, and its composition and reception enabled Wollstonecraft to rebuild her life and re-enter the world.

This background was unknown to the first readers of *Letters Written in Sweden*, and in the book Wollstonecraft is careful to leave vague the precise nature of the business which dictates her wanderings. But on everything else she saw and thought while on her travels she is brilliantly and memorably precise. From the outset she makes it abundantly clear that she has no intention of being a whingeing travel writer who can find nothing more interesting to do than complain about the state of hotels. 'Travellers who require that every nation should resemble their native country', she writes with some robustness, 'had better stay at home.'

Having set out her vision of the kind of traveller she intends to be, Wollstonecraft proceeds to live up to her own ideals. She may at times be reduced to exhaustion by bumpy roads and lumpy mattresses but she is always alert to the strange beauty around her. In an early letter, as the rugged Swedish coast comes into view, she likens the prospect to seeing 'the bones of the world waiting to be clothed with every thing necessary to give life and beauty', a powerful image for an elemental, mysterious landscape.

Once ashore she finds much to say about the politics and social customs of the people she meets, and today her comments feel surprisingly contemporary. She is taken aback by the Swedish system of childrearing, which involves keeping children tucked up inside heated houses with little opportunity to run freely in the fresh air. The result, she writes, are children who 'appear to be nipt in the bud', denied the chance of an untrammelled, carefree existence even for a short period. She is more approving of Swedish laws concerning illegitimate offspring, which stipulate that both parents must contribute to the maintenance of the child, but she notes with regret that even this system only works when fathers acknowledge their responsibilities.

In Norway she describes with some relief a religious culture in which religious practice is kept in proportion and not allowed to become the preserve of blinkered hardliners. 'Aristocracy and fanaticism seem equally to be gaining ground in England . . . I saw very little of either in Norway.' Instead, while Norwegians go to church regularly, 'religion does not interfere with their employments'. In the Europe of the 1790s, brought to breaking-point by political fanaticism and political division, such moderation appears to her a revelation. Her travels lead her to conclude that it is zealots of all stripes who have wreaked destruction on Revolutionary France and her neighbours, and that greedy businessmen, political ideologues and an avaricious establishment all bear part of the blame. 'During my present journey, and whilst residing in France,' she concludes, 'I have had an opportunity of peeping behind the scenes of what are vulgarly termed great affairs, only to discover the mean machinery which has directed many transactions of moment. The sword has been merciful, compared with the depredations made on human life by contractors, and by the swarm of locusts who have battened on the pestilence they spread abroad.'

All this would be absorbing and fascinating in itself, but it doesn't take account of one very important element of *Letters Written in Sweden*. The thing that gives the book its heart is its form: these are letters written by a woman to the man she loves and who has betrayed her. Thrown on her own resources Wollstonecraft learns much about herself and she leaves her tale of self-discovery in the published version of her letters for all to see. 'I cannot immediately determine whether I ought to rejoice at having turned over in this solitude a new page in the history of my own heart,' she muses. Elsewhere she turns inward for comfort and emotional sustenance. 'I must fly from thought, and find refuge from sorrow in a strong imagination – the only solace for a feeling heart.' Reading this with the benefit of hindsight it is not hard to see why it had such an impact on Wordsworth and Coleridge, the great poets of the Romantic imagination.

The one thing that brings Wollstonecraft happiness on her travels is thoughts of Fanny, whom she has to leave in inns at various points when Imlay's business takes her to the most inhospitable corners of Scandinavia, but who nightly fills her dreams. 'I heard her sweet cooing beat on my heart from the cliffs, and saw her tiny footsteps on the sands.' It is, Wollstonecraft argues, a mighty responsibility to be the mother of a daughter in a world which systematically ignores the rights of women. 'I dread lest she should be forced to sacrifice her heart to her principles, or principles to her heart.' Yet despite the difficulties and dangers facing them both, Fanny offers the hope of a brighter future, and the restoration of happiness.

So *Letters Written in Sweden* touches on many things that feel astonishingly relevant today: a febrile Europe, gender politics, the responsibilities of parenthood, the possibilities of adventure and enquiry, the enduring fascination of foreign lands. Ultimately Wollstonecraft did find happiness, although her marriage to William Godwin was cut brutally short by her death in childbirth. And in spite of all the heartache, *Letters* is very far from being a melancholy book. Instead it is bold and brave and self-revealing, a testament to the resilience and creative power of its extraordinary author. Ultimately it exemplifies an age-old theme. As Wollstonecraft is restored to life by the act of composition, her neglected classic demonstrates just how powerfully writing and the imagination can heal the heart, and make a person whole.

DAISY HAY is the author of *Mr and Mrs Disraeli: A Strange Romance* and *Young Romantics: The Shelleys, Byron and Other Tangled Lives*. She feels very privileged to spend her working life surrounded by such a glorious cast of romantic Romantics and Victorians.

Raising the Dead

REBECCA WILLIS

Someone must have recommended it. Otherwise there's no way, twenty years ago, I'd have picked up an 880-page book about the French Revolution. Even a novel. But I did pick up Hilary Mantel's *A Place of Greater Safety* (1992), and I was immediately sucked into the vortex of this swirling, populous epic that animates one of history's greatest and bloodiest convulsions. My paperback bears the scars of my attention: the faded front cover is detached and veined with creases, the corners worn and blurred, the pages dog-eared and soft as cloth. The impact the book had on me in return feels almost as physical. Because history, until that point, had left me completely cold. With *A Place of Greater Safety*, it suddenly came to hot-blooded life and stepped right off the page.

At school, history seemed to be about dates and deals and dead men. I did not choose to study it for A-level. Instead I chose English, devouring literature in great long gulps, and from it I patched together a rather hazy picture of the past, just enough to provide a context for whatever I was studying and help make sense of it, but no more. I learned to infer history from the art and literature of the time, stepping gingerly around it but never quite looking it straight in the eye. In my head I developed a timeline upon which the markers were books and plays and paintings. Actual historical events could, if necessary, be slotted in alongside them. Thus the Spanish Armada was defeated at about the time Shakespeare was writing *Henry IV, Part One*.

Hilary Mantel, *A Place of Greater Safety* (1992)
Fourth Estate · Pb · 880pp · £9.99 · ISBN 9780007250554

The Battle of Waterloo took place in the same year that *Emma* was published. The French Revolution and William Blake's *Songs of Innocence* both saw the light of day in 1789. And so on. I'm not proud of this scheme or advocating it for others, but at the time it did seem to serve my (admittedly narrow) purposes.

So *A Place of Greater Safety* was a complete and utter revelation. In it we follow Camille Desmoulins, Georges-Jacques Danton and Maximilien de Robespierre from their births – in provincial homes, into families with various degrees of dysfunction – and on through their schooldays. We see them turning into young men and getting their first jobs, their characters taking shape and crystallizing. We watch their interlocking lives as the revolution swells and they rise to its surface, and we recognize them as if we've grown up with them: which, after several hundred pages, in a way we have. Never mind that much of the detail comes straight out of Mantel's prodigious imagination. I wanted to shout: 'You mean these dry, dead people made jokes and wept and made friends and flirted and made love and blasphemed?' Somehow, though it should be obvious, nothing before had ever made me *feel* that history was once life. Mantel's genius here – and later in *Wolf Hall* – is to make you care about her characters as if they were your intimates, even, or maybe especially, when they have few redeeming features.

It is largely their flaws that make the three protagonists so mesmerizing. Desmoulins and Robespierre meet as children at the Collège Louis-le-Grand in Paris, where they develop a loyal friendship based on their opposing natures. Desmoulins – mercurial, amoral, charming and sexually indiscriminate – becomes the radical pamphleteer with the silver pen who can inspire the crowds with his writings. On 12 July 1789 he leaps on to a table outside the Café du Foy and, losing his habitual stammer, makes an impassioned call to arms. Two days later the Bastille falls. Robespierre is the cold intellectual of the revolution: ascetic, self-controlled, purely rational. Nothing is known about his sex life, but Mantel gives him a secret one which, paradoxically, makes his chilling detachment as he escalates the Reign of Terror seem more credible.

Desmoulins also befriends Danton, a young barrister, and introduces him to Robespierre, then over the years acts as a go-between and peacemaker between the two politicians as they circle each other warily and eventually, fatally, fall out. Danton is a huge bear of a man with appetites to match and a scarred face. He's a natural leader and a rabble-rousing orator, full of bluff confidence and fearless drive, who also thinks he's above the law and has a habit of disappearing from Paris when things get too hot. In the National Convention he votes for the execution of Louis XVI, and as a member of the first Committee of Public Safety he effectively runs the country for a while. But by the time he realizes the killing is out of control, it is too late.

Robespierre, when power comes to him, makes Danton look moderate. In the end Danton and Desmoulins argue against him and the murderous excesses of the Terror. Robespierre shows a brief flicker of humanity when he tries to save his old schoolfriend, but then – after a trial without evidence or witnesses – he lets him go with Danton to the guillotine.

As the Revolution builds with the inexorable force of a tidal wave, the realization dawns on the protagonists that they can no longer control it and are standing directly in its devastating path. And by the end of the final chapter you, as the reader, sense – because by now you have understood the full implication of the word 'revolution' – that the wheel will keep turning and that Robespierre will not survive for long.

Historians can get quite hot under the collar about fiction being woven into the

Anna Trench

71

fabric of fact. But a friend who did a degree in the subject points out that history always employs the imagination. You have the source material, which may be more or less reliable and which you must evaluate, and these various sources are like dots on a page. Joining the dots is a creative act. As soon as you write one single sentence beyond what is precisely proven, you are adding something of yourself. Mantel adds a lot of herself; an academic might add the minimum. The different approaches, from the barest account to the most embellished retelling, exist on a spectrum. That, at any rate, is how I see it. To me *A Place of Greater Safety* has an emotional truth: it may not all be literally true, but it feels true, and it allows me access to a subject that, in its purest form, I couldn't digest.

It doesn't, anyway, pretend to be anything other than a novel. But I trust Mantel to have done her research, and she herself says that she never lets her version of events contradict the known facts. Where possible, she uses the historical figures' own words, from their writings or speeches. 'The reader may ask', she teases in her introduction, 'how to tell fact from fiction. A rough guide: anything that seems particularly unlikely is probably true.'

How history is made is one of the novel's themes: her three protagonists are conscious that they are making history and consider how posterity will view them. Desmoulins' wife Lucile writes an 'official' diary and also her brown notebooks which are for 'dark, precise thoughts: unpalatable thoughts' – two versions of the same life, reminding us that we can never know what historical figures were really thinking. How Mantel must have enjoyed closing the first chapter with a 1793 quotation from Robespierre: 'History is fiction.' Her book is a challenge to the dates-and-dead-men type of history, a gauntlet thrown defiantly down at the feet of the worthy textbook. The novel combines her wit and playfulness, her interrogation of her own methods, her constant but lightly worn cleverness, her profound sense of humanity, and it takes flight.

A Place of Greater Safety is even more fascinating today because it is so evidently the direct ancestor of *Wolf Hall*. The latter is a tighter construction, with a narrower focus, a more consistent style and a cast list of a mere 96 characters instead of 150, but the shared DNA is plain. In the earlier book you witness Mantel honing her skills, and you watch in slack-jawed awe as she marshals her material into a kaleidoscopic whole, blending fact and fiction, artfully juggling the various storylines at the same time as experimenting stylistically. She works to stop the vast surface of the novel becoming too uniform, ensuring it will snag your attention. The dialogue is snappy, and between scenes there may be a direct quotation from Robespierre's notebooks or she may throw in a list showing the rise in the price of household staples between 1785 and 1789 (the cost of firewood went up a whopping 91 per cent). Just when you have acclimatized to the omniscient narration, a character suddenly speaks in the first person. Some conversations are set down as if in a script for a film or a play. While this stylistic skittishness has irked some critics, I love the evanescent, glinting quality it gives to the book.

Above all, there is a scene in Robespierre's early childhood where the embryonic narrative voice of *Wolf Hall* can be fleetingly heard. In it, Mantel uses the pronoun 'he' for longer than is really comfortable, before telling us which character she is talking about. This signature of *Wolf Hall* – I don't know if it has a name, let's call it the 'third person obscure' – alienated some readers who never worked out that when she says 'he', unless it's clearly someone else, she is always referring to Cromwell. It is not a hollow trick: it enacts Cromwell's insinuating presence.

Both my children refused to specialize in history and my attempts to persuade them fell on deaf ears. I recognized their stance from my own childhood: what is interesting about dead people? What is the point of knowing about stuff that's already happened? Perhaps it is as much a characteristic of childhood to look forward as it is of old age to look back. At school, from the age of about 11 onwards, they'd been given raw source material and asked to work out which was more reliable: the account, for example, of someone who was present at the time but an enemy of the king, or an account written by a monk a century later. They didn't care. 'Ah,' said a history teacher of my acquaintance, 'they're trying to teach them to think like historians. But what makes history interesting at their age is the story: what's going to happen next?' It's not just at their age: some of us always want the story, and Mantel is a genius at spinning it.

REBECCA WILLIS has worked at *Vogue*, the *Independent on Sunday* and *Intelligent Life*, and is no longer afraid of history books.

Ian Stephens, 'Peewit',
wood engraving

A Purple Gentian

TANIA HERSHMAN

I once went to see a woman who was a sort of psychic and read the future through stones.

She arranged them on a tray and you put your feet into a tub of them. It sounds a little cuckoo, but she was delightful, in her eighties, laughed a great deal and kept chickens. Part of her routine was telling you which dead people wanted to say hello to you. She mentioned various people who didn't sound at all familiar, and I nodded politely. Then she said, 'There's someone here who looks a bit like Albert Einstein.' I said, 'Oh! Could it *be* Einstein?' She giggled and said, 'Yes, it could.' Then she said, 'He watches you a lot, and finds you amusing.'

Albert Einstein finds me amusing. This was the highlight of my day, my decade. You see, I have a bit of a crush on Einstein. I have two large posters of him; in one, in my study, he is saying, 'Imagination is more important than knowledge.' The one in my bedroom declares: 'I never said gravity was responsible for people falling in love.' I've also written several short stories featuring Einstein – so the idea that this might tickle him was rather wonderful.

I mention all this not to entertain you – well, not *just* to entertain you – but to explain how the whole damn thing started. I read *Einstein's Dreams* (1992), by Alan Lightman, not long after it was published. I was in my mid-twenties, freshly released from a degree in maths and physics I had understood very little of, and then a

Alan Lightman, *Einstein's Dreams* (1992)

Corsair · Pb · 144pp · £8.99 · ISBN 9781780335575

diploma in journalism. I wasn't a scientist, certainly not a physicist (I loved physics but just wasn't any good at it). I was working as a science journalist, but what I really wanted to write was fiction that somehow incorporated science. And Alan Lightman was the first author I'd come across who did this, beautifully.

Lightman is a former astrophysicist, now a professor of science and writing at MIT. *Einstein's Dreams* was his first book-length work. In a nutshell, it is his fantasy of what Einstein might have been dreaming about as he formulated his Theory of Relativity. For those of you without physics qualifications, here's the gist: Einstein demonstrated that time is not fixed, it's relative. During our degree, we undergraduates found Relativity so baffling that the lecturer used to stop midway and tell jokes to break it all up. Basically, it's about getting over-long cars into too-short garages, and one twin being younger than the other when returning from space, and so on . . .

In fact the easiest way to explain it is this: a person who is moving will observe things differently from someone who is standing still. In fact, 'still' and 'moving' are relative, as becomes clear when you're on a stationary train and the train next to you moves. So, if for a person on the street two things happen simultaneously (someone throws an orange in the air while someone else sneezes), a person on a bus might see the person sneeze first, then the orange ascend, because her frame of reference is different.

Anyway, the crux is this: time is flexible, and Lightman let his imagination take flight in order to explore other concepts of time that Einstein may have contemplated on the way to his theory.

But this glorious book – which really isn't a novel, despite the publisher's insistence – contains all of life in its thirty sections, each of which is a short story illustrating a different theory of time, interspersed with three interludes involving Einstein and his friend Besso, and a prologue and an epilogue.

As befits a scientist, the book is rigidly structured: a prologue, eight stories, then an interlude, another eight stories, another interlude, eight more stories, a third interlude, then a final six stories. (Is there some mathematical significance to all this? Very likely!) The edition I have, from 1994, is also a physically small, almost square, pocket-sized book, with delightfully ragged edges.

The book is set in Bern, where Einstein was living and working as a patent clerk. The short stories are untitled, but dated – from 14 April 1905 to 28 June 1905 – as if they are field reports. (Einstein's paper on Special Relativity was published on 30 June 1905, just one of four papers he published that year.) All the stories involve unnamed Swiss villagers and townspeople.

We begin with a prologue, which starts thus:

> In some distant arcade, a clock tower calls out six times and then stops. The young man slumps at his desk. He has come to the office at dawn, after another upheaval. His hair is uncombed and his trousers are too big. In his hand he holds twenty crumpled pages, his new theory of time, which he will mail today to the German journal of physics . . . In the dim light that seeps through the room, the desks appear shadowy and soft, like large sleeping animals . . .

This opening, taken together with the title of the book, gives the reader an excellent impression of what is to come. The language is poetic, yet we are immediately introduced to the notion of time and the framework of physics – and to the man himself, young and dishevelled. The atmosphere is dreamlike; we are very firmly not in the stereotypical world of science, with its rationality, its tangibles and equations. Boundaries are blurred; we are on that border between sleep and wakefulness.

The first story, '14 April 1905', plunges us straight in: 'Suppose time is a circle, bending back on itself.' The second story begins: 'In this world, time is like a flow of water, occasionally displaced by a bit of debris, a passing breeze.' But not all the stories begin in the same way – and, contrary to what you might expect, this is not science fiction, not in the traditional sense. Each short story is a different world, but Lightman's genius, for me anyway, is that he uses us humans and this life, with all its joys and tragedies, to illustrate thirty different approaches to time.

For example, in a world where there are two times, mechanical time ('rigid and metallic') and body time ('squirms and wriggles like a bluefish in a bay'), Lightman reflects us back at ourselves: 'Many are convinced that mechanical time does not exist . . . They do not keep clocks in their houses. Instead, they listen to their heartbeats . . . Then, there are those who think their bodies don't exist. They live by mechanical time. They rise at seven o'clock in the morning . . . They make love between eight and ten at night.'

Love comes up often in these stories; I guess love and time are inextricably linked. But what Lightman does, in fact, is to show how time – and how we feel about time – is linked to everything: pain, doubt, uncertainty, truth, humour, hope, knowledge, science, philosophy, beauty, what it means to be human. He doesn't pull his punches; he is clearly on the side of those who live by body time, for instance, the people who understand that whatever time is doing, each drop of it is precious.

One of the most beautiful scenes comes in a story in which everyone knows on precisely which day the world will end:

One minute before the end of the world, everyone gathers on the grounds of the Kunstmuseum. Men, women and children form a giant circle and hold hands. No one moves. No one speaks . . . This is the last minute of the world. In the absolute silence a purple gentian in the garden catches the light on the underside of its blossom, glows for a moment, then dissolves among the other flowers.

I learned so much from this book. It filled me with wonder, it added poetry and dreaming to my notions of science, it opened me up to other ways of noticing what is happening around me. *Einstein's*

Dreams was the start of a journey that I am still on – I am midway through a PhD in creative writing and am taking inspiration from particle physics – and I can't recommend it highly enough. At the end of the book, Einstein 'feels empty, and he stares without interest at the tiny black speck and the Alps'. I think Lightman is saying that if we stop dreaming, this is what happens.

Einstein never stopped. Were he watching me write this, he might smile and nod, and, I hope, feel that in some tiny and most ungenius-like way I'm carrying on his legacy. Or, at the very least, I'm making him chuckle, which is just as good.

TANIA HERSHMAN tries at every opportunity to squeeze some science into her fiction and poetry and to persuade others to do so – despite her early traumatic experiences. She is the author of two short-story collections: see www. taniahershman.com.

Anna Trench

Land of Lost Content

MARTIN SORRELL

One afternoon sometime in the early 1950s, the lad who by a country mile was my father's ablest pupil in his sixth-form French and Spanish class rang our doorbell, and announced that the schoolgirl on his arm had just consented to become his wife. Not immediately, of course, but as soon as both had made it through the higher education which would force them to live far from each other for the next three or four years. That lad was Ted Walker, his bride-to-be Lorna Benfell. The two had met when he was 14, she one year older. They'd fallen urgently in love. Ted wanted my parents to be among the first to hear. He held them both in high regard, and they him – a mutual affection that lasted to the end.

Ted and Lorna ticked off the years, months, days, until in 1956 they were married. All this is recorded in Ted's first memoir, *The High Path*, which was reissued as a Slightly Foxed Edition in 2010.

There is, however, a sequel to *The High Path*. For better, for worse, the marriage stayed its course through thick and sometimes wafer thin, down to the years of Lorna's illness and her shocking death in 1987. *The Last of England*, Ted's second memoir – a copy of which he inscribed to my parents, as he had the first, and which, pristine in its

---

Ted Walker, *The Last of England* (1993), is out of print. However a handful of copies of his first memoir, *The High Path* (224pp), are still available from Slightly Foxed in a limited and numbered cloth-bound pocket edition (subscriber price: UK & Eire £16, Overseas £18; non-subscriber price: UK & Eire £17.50, Overseas £19.50). All prices include post and packing.

dust-jacket enriched by Ford Madox Brown's celebrated painting, has been handed down to me – is the account of those final years, of pain and of love lost and won: love between Ted and Lorna, reignited in her decline; love of an England gone for good; the healing love of another country; and love reborn in a new marriage.

A few weeks after burying Lorna in their local churchyard, a distracted Ted took himself off to Spain. He couldn't bear to linger in his haunted house; in fact he didn't want to be anywhere at all in England. He packed necessities into his little Fiat, locked up and fled. He drove all the way through France, over the Pyrenees, then down to the villa he'd been lent in Andalusia. The idea was to immerse himself in different sounds, colours, smells. He'd swap the mists of England for the pitiless sun and the harsh aesthetics of gipsy music and bullfights that had beguiled him many years before. The rough beauty of the Spanish language, so removed from English, would reopen some forgotten pathways in his brain, and he'd be a changed person.

At one point during his stay, his daughter Susan visited, and as Ted sat waiting for her in a bar at Malaga airport, he spilled a little red wine on the white tablecloth. The blot spread, and he recalled the morning when a tiny spot of blood had appeared overnight on Lorna's pillow. They'd concluded that probably it was no more than a mild nose bleed, and had dismissed it from their thoughts. That morning was in the very late 1970s, around the time Margaret Thatcher began to dismantle what Ted loved about England.

I stress England, not because Ted had any disregard for Britain's other constituents, but because he didn't feel for them the umbilical attachment he had to England. It was a deep-veined, viscerally left-wing, Billy Bragg attachment, inherited from his father, a skilled carpenter, who'd motorcycled – his own word was 'bladdered', as Ted notes in *The High Path* – down to the south coast from Birmingham during the early 1930s to look for work. He and his wife had settled in a small house alongside a trunk road in Lancing, a house which,

J.Weston Lewis

when I visited it after Ted's death in 2004, had become so forlorn that it was demolished shortly after. It was there, by the grinding A259, in that least genteel part of Sussex, that Ted grew up, within sight of the Channel, the River Adur and the Downs, all subjects of the beautiful verse that makes him one of the great nature poets of the post-war generation.

The dab of blood on the pillow was fateful, the first evidence of the drama building up inside Lorna's head. It didn't take long for them to realize that it spelled big trouble, and indeed, after a succession of tests and scans, the grim truth was revealed. The 'bud of a dark, diabolical rose', as Ted calls it, was opening behind the bridge of Lorna's nose. The cancer worsened remorselessly through the Thatcher decade, and necessitated the removal of Lorna's right eye and part of her upper jawbone before it had finished its grisly work.

Ted was mourning well before Lorna's body gave up. It must be extraordinarily difficult to find the words that match grief, but being a fine poet is a great help. Douglas Dunn, for one, achieves it in *Elegies*. Ted claimed that the Muse had long since deserted him, but she can only have been hiding. The poet in him is alive on most pages of *The Last of England*'s carefully crafted prose. To my mind, the book is at its best not so much in the descriptions of Lorna's ravaged condition as in the evocations of the world that she, then Ted, were going to lose.

Emotions are transposed from the medical horrors, and explode in the remembrance of rural England: the Chilterns, the Cotswolds, the Vale of the White Horse, the Kentish Weald and particularly Sussex, whose loveliness is conjured on to pages filled with 'blues, yellows . . . delicately pararhyming light greens' – nuanced tones of the county Ted loved above all others. He writes wonderful sentences on the majesty of beeches; there's a lament for Chanctonbury Ring's land-mark trees, felled by the Great Storm of 1987; recollections of blackberry lanes and bluebell woods by Elgar's cottage; enduring echoes of the cello concerto's *rubato* melancholy. And one Sussex piece of man-made beauty is admired, unnamed but obviously the King Edward VII Hospital near Midhurst, where Lorna was sent for some hopeless tests, and to which, a couple of years ago, deviating from our route home, my wife guided me. She wanted to show me the Lutyens-style buildings, the Gertrude Jekyll gardens, the view towards the Downs, fillips to her dejected soul during some trau-matic childhood weeks there.

After Lorna's death, Ted stalled, utterly benumbed. But his three months in Spain cranked him back to life. He did a bit of writing, he corrected some proofs, he walked, he swam, he drank in *bodegas* with new acquaintances. Activities that took him out of himself and gave him enough courage to face the future, which involved first of all coming back home. But as he set foot in England again, it hit him like a *banderilla* in a bullfight that it wasn't the country for him. Sooner or later, he would have to leave for good. The die had been cast.

But then things took an unexpected turn. By a most painful coin-cidence, two dear friends of Ted and Lorna's had been going through a wretched drama of their own in the final months of Lorna's life. The wife, Audrey, lost her husband almost at the same time Ted lost Lorna. They became each other's solace. They wept together, took walks together, cooked for each other, and of course they talked. After a year of soul-searching, hesitation, lows and highs, they decided to get married and, with timely discretion, their several ghosts beat a retreat.

The newly-weds reclaimed Argyll House, Ted and Lorna's last home, in Eastergate, near Chichester, and were living there in 1997 when I met Ted for the second and last time. He'd suggested lunch in his favourite pub, the Black Horse at nearby Binsted. I found him sitting at the bar, finishing a whisky and lining up another (that much *The Last of England* had prepared me for). He was dapper and urbane, not the rugged countryman I'd expected. He spoke of my father, whose funeral he was upset to have missed as he'd been on a lecture tour of Australia at the time. I conveyed my mother's warm greetings and her standing offer of tea should he find himself in her neighbourhood.

We talked of poetry, his of course. I asked what he thought lay ahead for him. New poems? Another book about Spain? More short stories for *The New Yorker*? We'll see, he said, but first he and Audrey had to move. It was high time. They were too close to pain, theirs and others'. Besides, *that woman* had completely finished England off. Spain beckoned, and not long after I heard that Ted and Audrey had bought a house a few kilometres inland from Alicante. It was there, one spring evening in 2004, as he was cooking a supper of *riñones al jerez*, that Ted collapsed, and was rushed to hospital in Valencia, where he died a few hours later. His body was returned to Sussex. He lies side by side with Lorna in the churchyard a mile from their last home.

The Last of England turned out to be almost the last of Ted Walker. It's a message of farewell to England: it's a love letter to an unheard, absent wife: and it's a threnody for himself.

MARTIN SORRELL's feature on Ted Walker's poetry, entitled *Walker of the Downs*, was broadcast on BBC Radio 4 in 2009.

Not-so-gay Paree

ROWENA MACDONALD

I first read Jean Rhys in my mid-teens; a copy of *Quartet* from my parents' bookshelf, which drew me with its undemanding slimness and its cover featuring the beautiful face of Isabelle Adjani in soft focus above a chessboard with the heads of Maggie Smith and Alan Bates floating around her. (The three starred in the Merchant Ivory film of the book, which I have never seen.) From the back cover I learned it was set amid 'the winter-wet streets of Montparnasse, Pernods in smoke-filled cafés [and] . . . cheap hotel rooms with mauve-flowered wallpaper'. Chic Parisian misery: just what teenage girls love.

The contents did not disappoint. The first lines read:

> It was about half-past five on an October afternoon when Marya Zelli came out of the Café L'Avenue . . . She had been sitting there for nearly an hour and a half, and during that time she had drunk two glasses of black coffee, smoked six caporal cigarettes and read the week's *Candide*.

So glamorous. I was immediately plunged into pre-war Left Bank bohemia; a world of painters, writers and artist's models, 'gaily dressed little prostitutes' and beautiful young men with powdered faces. The mood, rather than the plot or characters, stayed with me. Rhys is brilliant at conveying melancholy in an aesthetic way, so that

Jean Rhys, *Quartet* (1928) · Penguin · Pb · 160pp · £12.99 · ISBN 9780141183923; and *Voyage in the Dark* (1934) · Penguin · Pb · 176pp · £8.99 · ISBN 9780141183954.

even though *Quartet* is a sad tale, Marya's suffering is leavened by the romance of her surroundings: 'the pavements were slippery and glistening, with pools of water here and there, sad little mirrors which the reflections of the lights tinted with a dull point of red. The trees along the Boulevard Clichy stretched ridiculously frail and naked arms to a sky without stars.'

Jean Rhys's first four novels, published between 1928 and 1939, were all heavily autobiographical. *Quartet* (first published under the title *Postures*) is based on the love triangle between Rhys, Ford Madox Ford and his wife Stella Bowen, an Australian artist. Ford and Bowen looked after Rhys while her second husband was in prison for entering France without valid papers. Rhys was frail, poverty-stricken and ineffectual. Throughout her life she lived, like Blanche DuBois, on 'the kindness of strangers'. The Fords bailed her out financially and invited her to stay with them. Bowen painted her, and Ford encouraged her to write.

Unsurprisingly, Ford's interest was not entirely altruistic and they had an affair. Bowen was aware of it and tacitly accepting; it seems she hoped it would, like Ford's previous affairs, run its course. An objective observer might consider Bowen the wronged party but Rhys, who was unfailingly self-pitying, depicts herself as the victim in *Quartet*. Marya is a fragile, highly strung, childlike figure, at the mercy of the controlling Heidler and his wife Lois. They take her over, try to stop her visiting her husband in prison and insist she doesn't make an embarrassing fuss when Heidler ends the affair. Their wealth gives them power, and Marya feels she is treated as a quasi-prostitute who must service Heidler's sexual needs in return for bed and board, and not expect him to leave his wife.

Lois is, in Marya's eyes, 'formidable' and 'insensitive to the point of stupidity': the kind of person who likes to keep her enemies close.

She didn't analyse; she didn't react violently; she didn't go in for absurd generosities or pities. Her motto was: 'I don't think

women ought to make nuisances of themselves. I don't make a
nuisance of myself; I grin and bear it, and I think that other
women ought to grin and bear it too.'

She is, as Marya mockingly notes, 'obviously of the species wife'.
The Heidlers think of themselves as 'excessively modern' but to Marya
they are laughably bourgeois, precursors of the chattering classes,
temporarily slumming it in Montparnasse:

> You talk and you talk and you don't understand . . . It's all false,
> all second-hand. You say what you've read and what other
> people tell you. You think you're very brave and sensible, but
> one flick of pain to yourself and you'd crumple up.

On rereading *Quartet* twenty-five years later I am struck by how
annoyingly passive Marya is, and how much sympathy I feel for Lois,
neither of which I remember feeling on first reading; but perhaps as
a teenager I was more kindly disposed towards suffering heroines,
especially if they suffered so stylishly.

At university, where I studied English, *Wide Sargasso Sea*, Rhys's
last novel, published in 1966, was on the curriculum. Everyone loved
it. The orthodoxy is that this is her masterpiece. It is undeniably
beautiful and more ambitious than her slim volumes set in Paris and
London but it never touched me as much – it seems less personal to
Rhys and doesn't have quite the same coolly economical prose.

A couple of years after graduating I went to Montreal with a
friend, who knew someone there who would put us up. For a year I
lived there illegally, working 'under the table' as a waitress, bartender
and life model. To begin with, everything was exciting and vivid and
I felt creatively inspired. I was living on the Plateau, just off St
Laurent Boulevard, which back then was cheap, scruffy and alive
with artistic activity. When I wasn't working I was trying to write and
getting involved with unsuitable men.

The adventure began to pall after about nine months and it's at this point, judging from the date written inside the front cover, that I read *Voyage in the Dark* (1934), Rhys's third novel, about her time as a chorus girl in London in her late teens. Rhys was new to England. To someone who had spent the first sixteen years of her life on the Caribbean island of Dominica, the cold, grey weather and, as she saw them, cold, grey people came as a shock. *Voyage in the Dark* describes the journey from innocence to experience of Rhys's alter ego, Anna Morgan, who joins a theatre company that travels the provinces: 'I got used to everything except the cold and that the towns we went to always looked so exactly alike . . . rows of little houses with chimneys like the funnels of dummy steamers and smoke the same colour as the sky'.

Like Marya in *Quartet* – like all Rhys's protagonists, in fact – Anna is ultra-feminine, passive and desperate for a man to look after her. She's infuriatingly unfeminist but obviously of her time, and Rhys captures atmospherically the precarious, often vertiginously fearful existence of a lone woman cut off from her family and the safety net of conventional life. While I would never have admitted to wanting a man to protect me in Montreal, I certainly identified with Anna's loneliness and homesickness. I also recognized the freedom Anna feels in a new country where no one knows her.

Voyage in the Dark is not unrelenting in its gloom, at least not at the start. Anna enjoys the camaraderie of the other chorus girls, and the nights out when she's wined and dined by louche men in 'swanky clubs', although, as she says, 'in my heart I was always sad, with the same sort of hurt that the cold gave me in my chest'. She meets a kindly man, whom she hopes will be her rescuer, but he breaks off their relationship at the encouragement of his cousin, who feels she is not respectable enough. Her finances become more desperate and she drifts into working as a prostitute – as Jean Rhys did briefly – in a brothel masquerading as a manicurist's in Camden Town. She gets pregnant and the novel concludes with her floating in and out of consciousness as she undergoes a backstreet abortion.

I returned to England shortly after reading *Voyage in the Dark* and had a miserable few months back with my parents, trying to restart my life. Unable to get a job, I moved to London, slept on a friend's floor and started temping. I began to write stories about Montreal, about the characters I'd met while waitressing and life modelling. I wanted to capture the feeling of being young and adrift in a foreign city and, as Jean Rhys did with Paris, the intoxicating demi-mondaine atmosphere of Montreal.

Only unscrupulous places would employ staff cash-in-hand so I worked in some real dives for terrible bosses. The people I worked with were often economic migrants from Haiti or Turkey or refugees from war-torn countries in the Middle East. An overarching theme began to emerge in my stories, of the way a city can force people, like Anna in *Voyage in the Dark*, from innocence into experience, from 'green' to 'smoked meat' – the title of my first collection of short stories, which also refers to Montreal's signature dish. My characters never plumb such depths as Anna did but I hope I've captured that sense of possibility that Anna occasionally feels: the times, as she says, 'when a fine day, or music, or looking in the glass and thinking I was pretty, made me start again imagining that there was nothing I couldn't do, nothing I couldn't become'.

ROWENA MACDONALD's *Smoked Meat* was shortlisted for the 2012 Edge Hill Prize. She has won a number of prizes, and was runner-up in the Royal Society of Literature's V. S. Pritchett Prize, 2013. She is currently finishing a novel.

Caught in the Act

DEREK PARKER

I waited until my wife was looking the other way, nipped quickly in and bought it. Admittedly, it weighed six pounds, its heavy leather binding was rather battered and, as the label said, it 'lacks part of brass lock'; but it was irresistible, even at £50 – once clearly irresistible, too, to His Majesty King Edward VII, a collection of dukes and duchesses, and 'the whole of the leading members of the theatrical profession', all of whom had been 'pleased to subscribe, in advance of publication'.

The latter group provides the clue, of course. *The Stage in the Year 1900* is 'a de luxe souvenir, being a collection of photogravure plates portraying the leading players and playwrights of the day and a history of the stage during the Victorian era'. I'm perfectly aware that such a book is only likely to appeal to someone besotted with the theatre and the fusty glamour of stages on which the curtain has long since fallen for ever. It's just that I simply can't help being one of them.

I'm also aware that it's one of those books which surely define the word 'obscure'. But what pleasure we can get from obscure books – in this case meeting from the thick matt pages the stern gazes of Sir Squire Bancroft and Mr Beerbohm Tree, the keen glance of the wonderfully handsome Lewis Waller and the mournful stare of the great comedian Charles Hawtrey. The ladies, too, send their greetings in stately, melting gazes – Miss Julia Neilson ('a celebrated Princess Pannonia in *The Princess and the Butterfly*'), Miss Ellen Terry ('her name is known wherever the English language is spoken') and Mrs Langtry, in an alarming hat, 'whose beauty and personal charm have fascinated playgoers both in England and America'. No prizes for guessing where King Edward left his bookmark.

The pleasure of obscure books lies partly in the belief that almost no one else possesses or wants to possess them – at least, that is how it seems; otherwise, surely, they would not have lurked so long in the murky corners of second-hand bookshops. It was, of all places, in a second-hand bookshop in Australia's Blue Mountains that I picked up a book published in London in 1810: *The Lives of Andrew Robinson Bowes, Esq., and the Countess of Strathmore* by Jesse Foot, Esq., Surgeon. It was clearly worth a look, if only for the villainous frontispiece portrait of Bowes, and it turned out to be obscure not only in itself (does *anyone* else have a copy?) but also in the story it told of the wooing and abduction of the richest heiress in early nineteenth-century Britain, the Countess of Strathmore (the present Queen's great-great-great-grandmother). She was handsome and intelligent but fell prey to a seducer of the first order. Stoney Bowes married her for her fortune; was furious when she declined to sign it over; beat her up and made off with her to the north where he imprisoned her; and when rescue threatened carried her on horseback over frozen fields and icy ditches before their capture and her escape.

She saw her husband brought to trial (Horace Walpole among the fascinated onlookers) and Bowes came to a Bad End, with a minor part in literary history as the inspiration for Thackeray's Barry Lyndon – the author heard the story from the Countess's grandson, thirty years after the events. Almost a century and a half later, Foot's obscure book prompted me to research the story further and write my own account of it. The most obscure book can sometimes earn its place.

Probably more obscure even than Foot's volume, and I suspect even less likely to be on any other shelf except perhaps that of the British Library, is *Representative Actors: a collection of criticisms, anecdotes, personal descriptions, etc., etc., referring to many Celebrated*

British Actors from the Sixteenth to the Present Century; with Notes, memoirs, and a short account of English acting, published in 1850 by one William Clark Russell. I have no idea who he was, but he was clearly as besotted by actors and acting as I, and his book is crammed with irresistibly fascinating facts and anecdotes.

What would one give to have seen Ned Kynaston? When Pepys saw him perform twice in the same week, once in a male and once in a female role, he pronounced him the prettiest woman and the handsomest man in the whole house. Colley Cibber, the manager and playwright, remarked that Kynaston 'was so beautiful a youth that the ladies of quality prided themselves in taking him with them in their coaches to Hyde Park in his theatrical habit, after the play'. Kynaston appeared in petticoats even after Nell Gwynn and other women had taken to the stage – it was he who held up the start of a performance attended by Charles II who, when he enquired the reason for the delay, was told that 'the queen was not shaved yet'.

A century later, Peg Woffington was a beautiful actress, one of whose greatest successes was *en travestie* as Sir Harry Wildair in Farquhar's *The Constant Couple.* She was not celebrated for sexual reticence. When, after one performance as Wildair, she remarked, 'In my conscience, I believe half the men in the audience take me for one of their own sex,' another actress replied, 'It may be so; but in my conscience, the other half can convince them to the contrary.'

Poverty then as now stalked the profession, and most actors bore the inevitable with an often witty shrug of the shoulders. When Ned Shuter (who created the roles of Mr Hardcastle in *She Stoops to Conquer* and Sir Anthony Absolute in *The Rivals*) was rebuked by a friend with, 'Aren't you ashamed to appear in the street with twenty holes in your stockings? – why don't you get them mended?' the fine comic actor replied, 'No, my friend. I am above it; better have twenty holes than one darn . . . a hole is the accident of the day, but a darn is *premeditated poverty.*'

The writers whom WCR quotes do their best to describe the

quality of their subjects' acting but, then as now, that was notoriously difficult to convey. The best most people could do was in the line of one of Sam Rogers's dinner guests, who asked about the great Garrick. Rogers replied: '"Well, sir, *off* the stage he was a mean sneaking little fellow. But *on* the stage" – throwing up his hands and eyes – "oh, my great God!"' Mrs Clive, who often appeared with Garrick, 'was one night seen standing at the wing, weeping and scolding alternately at his acting. Angry at last at finding herself so affected, she turned on her heel, crying, "D—— him, he could act *a grid-iron!*"'

George III and Prinny were both avid theatregoers, though the latter 'could not bear the harrowing of the heart that Kean's Othello gave him'. His father once took Queen Charlotte to Covent Garden to see John Henderson in a melodrama, *The Mysterious Husband*. In the last act the hero dies, and Henderson was clearly too good: 'Charlotte,' exclaimed His Majesty, 'don't look – it's too much to bear!'

WCR pays some attention to backstage matters, quite properly, and celebrates one or two scene-painters and prompters. He quotes George Colman on the legendary Johnstone, who worked at Drury Lane. Johnstone was much occupied at Christmas time ensuring that the Lane's pantomime was more spectacular than Covent Garden's. One year a friend got him into the dress rehearsal at the Garden, where among the attractions of the Christmas foolery a *real* elephant was introduced. In due time the unwieldy brute came clumping down the stage, making a prodigious figure in a procession. The friend jogged Johnstone's elbow, whispering: 'This is a bitter bad job for Drury. Why, the elephant's *alive!* – he'll carry all before him. What d'ye think on't, eh?' 'Think on't!' said Johnstone, in a tone of the utmost contempt; 'I should be very sorry if I couldn't make a much better elephant than that at any time.'

I could go on – but I mustn't. All things – all actors – must come to an end. A Mr Norris died on stage in 1776. Twelve years later his wife, known as Mrs Barry, was appearing in Nicholas Rowe's *The Fair*

Penitent in the town in which he had died. In the last act, her character, Calista, had to lay her hand upon a skull. When she did so, she was immediately struck by an intense feeling of horror, and had to be carried to her lodging. Next day she made enquiries – and yes, dear reader, the skull was her husband's. She died within six weeks.

B. Lodge

I still haunt second-hand booksellers and charity shops, ever open to the temptations of the unfinished memoirs of Arthur Quiller-Couch, de Lauze's *Dancing and Deportment* (1623), Ronald Firbank's *Odette d'Antrevernes*, the *Dictionary of the Vulgar Tongue* (1811), *A Prognostication, of right good effect, contayninge playne, briefe, pleafant, chofen rules to iudge the wether for euer* by Leonard Digges (1555, but alas a nineteenth-century reprint). Obscure? – yes, but how helpful: 'Sunne beames fpottid, grene, pale or blacke fignifie rayne') . . .

DEREK PARKER lives in Sydney with his wife and two wirehaired terriers. His account of the adventures of Mary Eleanor Bowes, *The Trampled Wife* (2006), is readily available from good bookshops.

Bibliography

A Gift Subscription to *Slightly Foxed*

'My wife gave me an introductory subscription to Slightly Foxed. *I love it to bits and am now going to pay for the sub myself. In fact I have made a solemn and binding promise to continue it permanently!'*

So writes our subscriber Mr Hayes from Essex. We find that quite often happens – you give someone a subscription to *SF* and at the end of the year they can't bear the thought of being without it and decide to continue it themselves.

We're wondering if there are keen readers among your near and dear who you feel would enjoy a gift subscription. If so why not take the plunge and introduce them to *Slightly Foxed?* We'll send it to them elegantly wrapped and tied in ribbon with an accompanying card. It's a present that gives pleasure all year round – and if you're enjoying *Slightly Foxed* yourself, it's a great way of helping spread the word.

COMING ATTRACTIONS

MICHAEL HOLROYD is intrigued by a fatal love affair · ALISON LIGHT reports to *The Barracks* · WILLIAM PALMER examines *Zeno's Conscience* · SARAH PERRY follows the fortunes of the Cazalets · ANTHONY GARDNER explores *The Business of Loving* · MELISSA HARRISON meets the young Antonia White · ANDREW NIXON drops in on Mapp and Lucia · ISABEL LLOYD follows *The Way of an Actor*